McGRAW-HILL READING

Grammar

Grade 4

Practice Book

McGraw-Hill
School Division
New York   Farmington

CONTENTS

Justin and the Best Biscuits in the World

Just a Dream

Leah's Pony

Baseball Saved Us

Will Her Native Language Disappear?

The Hatmaker's Sign

Pat Cummings: My Story

Grass Sandals: The Travels of Basho

A Place Called Freedom

Twisted Trails

Scruffy: A Wolf Finds His Place in the Pack

Gluskabe and the Snow Bird

Meet an Underwater Explorer

On the Bus With Joanna Cole

Earth's First Creatures

The Fox and the Guinea Pig

Mom's Best Friend

The Rajah's Rice

Yeh-Shen: A Cinderella Story From China

Can We Rescue The Reefs?

Teammates

The Malachite Palace

The Toothpaste Millionaire

Whales

Saving the Everglades

Sentences

> • A **sentence** is a group of words that expresses a complete thought.
>
> • A **sentence fragment** is a group of words that does not express a complete thought.
>
> • Every sentence begins with a capital letter.
>
> • A **statement** is a sentence that tells something. It ends with a period.
>
> • A **question** is a sentence that asks something. It ends with a question mark.

Decide if each group of words makes a sentence. If it does, rewrite the sentence adding a capital letter and a period or a question mark.

1. it was too hot outside————————————

2. dad and Luke left in the morning

_____

3. when they hiked to Lost Lake

_____

4. dad went up the trail ————————————

5. a mountain that no one else knew about

_____

6. did they find a new "lost lake"

_____

Extension: Have students write two statements and two questions about an outdoor adventure.

1

Types of Sentences

> • A **statement** is a sentence that tells something. It ends with a period.
>
> • A **question** is a sentence that asks something. It ends with a question mark.
>
> • A **command** tells or asks someone to do something. It ends with a period.
>
> • An **exclamation** shows strong feeling. It ends with an exclamation mark.

Write **statement** if the sentence tells something. Write **question** if the sentence asks something. Write **command** if the sentence tells or asks someone to do something. Write **exclamation** if the sentence shows strong feeling. Then put the correct end mark at the end of each sentence.

1. Dad and Luke hiked to Lost Lake

_____

2. What did they find when they got there

_____

3. Put your pack on and let's go

_____

4. Luke wanted to camp by the creek

_____

5. Look out for bears

_____

6. How did they find their special lake

_____

Extension: Have students think of a special place. Then have them write a statement, a question, a command, and an exclamation about it.

Write Sentences

Rewrite each sentence. Correct the sentence capitalization and punctuation.

1. have you ever hiked in the mountains.

_____

2. try to imagine what it would be like?

_____

3. wouldn't it be great to sleep outdoors.

_____

4. put on your hiking boots?

_____

5. let's hit the trail?

_____

6. we can reach the lake by nightfall

_____

7. shall we make camp on the shore.

_____

8. i love the water.

_____

Extension: Have pairs of students choose a subject and take turns making up sentences about it. After each sentence, the student who is listening tells what kind of sentence it is.

Using Capital Letters and End Marks

- Every sentence begins with a capital letter.

- A **statement** ends with a period.

- A **question** ends with a question mark.

- A **command** ends with a period.

- An **exclamation** ends with an exclamation mark.

Correct each sentence by changing any incorrect lower case letters to capital letters and by adding the correct end mark. Use the line provided for your answers.

1. the lake was high in the mountains _____

2. how long did it take them to find it _____

3. it wasn't the lake Dad remembered _____

4. it was too crowded _____

5. dad would never stay there _____

6. they kept hiking until they found a special place _____

7. why was he different in the mountains _____

8. recall the things he did _____

4

Extension: Have pairs of students look through books and magazines for examples of statements, questions, commands, and exclamations and copy an example of each.

Book 4 / Unit 1
The Lost Lake
8

Kinds of Sentences

A. Decide if the sentence is a statement, a question, a command, or an exclamation. Write what type of sentence it is, and add the correct end mark on the line.

1. Luke was staying with his Dad —————————————

2. What did he do all day —————————————

3. Think about hiking —————————————

4. Where would you like to go —————————————

5. That sounds wonderful —————————————

B. Add the correct punctuation to each of these sentences.

6. I'll take a hiking trip in the mountains —————————————

7. You wake up and discover a lake —————————————

8. Do you think that would be exciting —————————————

9. I'd love to discover a lake —————————————

10. Could I name it after myself —————————————

Sentences and Punctuation Marks

- A **statement** is a sentence that tells something.

- A **question** is a sentence that asks something.

- A **command** tells or asks someone to do something.

- An **exclamation** shows strong feeling.

Mechanics

- Begin every sentence with a capital letter.

- A statement ends with a period.

- A question ends with a question mark.

- A command ends with a period.

- An exclamation ends with an exclamation mark.

Write each sentence correctly.

1. why did we wake up early

_____

2. we are going camping ——————————————————

3. it was a long hike to the lake

_____

4. we found it ——————————————————————

5. were there many people

_____

McGraw-Hill School Division

Sentence Subjects

Remind students that the subject of a sentence tells whom or what the sentence is about.

> - The **complete subject** includes all the words in the subject.
> - The **simple subject** is the main word in the complete subject. It tells exactly whom or what the sentence is about.
> - You can sometimes correct a sentence fragment by adding a subject.

Turn these sentence fragments into complete sentences by adding a subject.

1. Led to hard work

_____

2. Had to work too hard

_____

3. Wanted a place to come home to

_____

4. Found an accidental road

_____

5. Led through a meadow

_____

6. Stood at the end of the road

_____

7. Gave name tags to everyone

_____

8. Was full of "Amelia-things"

_____

Extension: Ask students to write sentences. Then have them exchange sentences with a partner and underline all the words that make up the subject.

Sentence Predicates

Remind students that the predicate of a sentence tells what the subject does or is.

- The **complete predicate** includes all the words in the predicate.

- The **simple predicate** is the main word in the complete predicate. It tells exactly what the subject does or is.

- You can sometimes correct a sentence fragment by adding a predicate.

Turn these fragments into complete sentences by adding a predicate.

1. Everyone in Amelia's family

_____

2. All the apples

_____

3. A white house with blue shutters

_____

4. An old shade tree

_____

5. Amelia's accidental road

_____

6. All the new children in class

_____

Extension: Ask students to write sentences. Then have them exchange sentences with a partner and underline all the words that make up the predicate.

Write Complete Sentences

- The **subject** of a sentence tells whom or what the sentence is about.
- The **predicate** of a sentence tells what the subject does or is.

Complete each sentence fragment. Then tell if you added a subject or a predicate.

1. Amelia and her family ————————————————

_____

2. Still felt sleepy ————————————————

_____

3. Drew a picture of a pretty white house ————————

_____

4. Everybody in the class ————————————————

_____

5. Danced for joy in the quiet meadow ————————

_____

6. A narrow, rocky footpath ————————————————

_____

Extension: Have students write the subject of a sentence and have a partner add a predicate to complete the sentence.

Sentence Punctuation

- A sentence begins with a capital letter.

- Sentences that make statements end with periods.

Read each group of words. If the words are a complete sentence, write a capital letter at the beginning and put a period at the end.

1. roads that led to strange places

_____

2. they pick peaches in June

_____

3. a neat white house with blue shutters

_____

4. the family followed the harvest

_____

5. now they picked apples

_____

6. her teacher never learned her name

_____

7. a rocky path through the meadow

_____

8. the old metal box was dented

_____

Extension: Have pairs of students take turns writing groups of words. The other partner must decide if the words are a sentence or a sentence fragment. If the words are a sentence fragment, the partner should add a subject or a predicate to complete the sentence.

Book 4 / Unit 1
Amelia's Road

McGraw-Hill School Division

Complete the Sentences

Circle the letter of the words that make each fragment a complete sentence.

1. drew a picture of a white house

   a with blue shutters

   b Amelia

   c with a yard

   d in school

2. Mrs. Ramos

   a Amelia's teacher

   b her teacher last year

   c at school

   d welcomed the new children

3. got up at dawn

   a Amelia's whole family

   b picking apples

   c before school started

   d still sleepy

4. The accidental road

   a a sturdy, old tree

   b was rocky and narrow

   c through a meadow

   d a shortcut to camp

5. Amelia's dream house

   a had a tree in the yard

   b someplace neat and tidy

   c anywhere in the world

   d something special

6. could be easily bruised

   a had to be careful

   b The ripe fruit

   c grabbed an apple

   d was ready to be picked

7. led from the highway to the tree

   a was a shortcut

   b through the meadow

   c The narrow path

   d went down a gentle hill

8. The farm workers

   a the apple harvest

   b were ready to move on

   c one more trip

   d sun-drenched fields

Subjects and Predicates

> • The **subject** of a sentence tells whom or what the sentence is about.
>
> • The **predicate** tells what the subject does or is.

Draw a line between the subject and the predicate in the following sentences.

1. Farm workers follow the crops.

2. Maps meant moving on to Amelia.

3. Amelia and her family pick apples.

4. They started working at dawn.

5. Mrs. Ramos gave Amelia's picture a red star.

6. Amelia's experiences at school made her happy.

7. The accidental road went through a meadow.

8. Amelia's special place was at the end of the road.

9. She buried her treasure box under the tree.

10. A hair ribbon, her name tag, and her picture were in the box.

Compound Sentences

> • A **conjunction** joins words or groups of words. *And*, *but*, and *or* are
>   conjunctions. Two related sentences can be joined with a comma and *and*,
>   *but*, or *or*.
>
> • A sentence that contains two sentences joined by *and, but,* or *or* is called a
>   **compound sentence**.

Add a comma and *and*, *but*, or *or*, and combine each pair of sentences into
one compound sentence.

1. The children laughed. The dogs barked.

_____

2. The chickens were not hungry. They still continued to eat.

_____

3. Get the animals in the barn. They'll be lost in the storm.

_____

4. Sarah had never driven a wagon. She was determined to learn.

_____

5. Caleb looked frightened. Anna covered her ears.

_____

6. They were afraid Sarah would leave. She came back.

_____

7. Sarah missed the sea. She would miss the family more.

_____

8. Caleb couldn't be pesky. Sarah would leave.

_____

McGraw-Hill School Division

8 Grade 4/Unit 1
Sarah, Plain and Tall

Extension: Have students write their own example of
a compound sentence.

13

Compound Subjects and Predicates

- You can combine two sentences by joining two subjects or two predicates with *and* or *or*.

- A **compound subject** contains two or more simple subjects that have the same predicate.

- A **compound predicate** contains two or more simple predicates that have the same subject.

Combine each pair of sentences to form one sentence using a compound subject or a compound predicate.

1. Papa could teach Sarah to drive the wagon. Caleb could, too.

_____

2. The dogs barked. They ran out to meet the wagon.

_____

3. The storm scattered the roses. It knocked over a tree.

_____

4. Papa plowed the field. Sarah plowed the field.

_____

5. Sarah had lived in Maine. She loved the sea.

_____

6. Seal ignored the storm. Sarah's chickens ignored the storm.

_____

7. Rose had a flower name. Violet had a flower name.

_____

8. Sarah drove to town. Sarah brought back presents.

_____

14

Extension: Have students write two sentences for a partner to combine into a sentence with a compound subject or predicate.

Grade 4/Unit 1
Sarah, Plain and Tall

/8

McGraw-Hill School Division

Write Sentences

Add *and*, *but*, or *or* to combine each pair of sentences into one sentence that is a compound sentence or has a compound subject or predicate.

1. Anna wanted Sarah to stay. Caleb wanted Sarah to stay.

_____

2. Sarah kissed everyone good-bye. Sarah drove away.

_____

3. Sarah ran out into the storm. Papa followed her.

_____

4. Thunder pounded. Lightning crackled.

_____

5. Seal curled up in my lap. Seal went to sleep.

_____

6. Sarah was just going shopping. The children did not know that.

_____

7. Nick jumped into the wagon. Nick sat beside Sarah.

_____

8. Papa will drive the wagon. Sarah will drive the wagon.

_____

8 Grade 4/Unit 1
Sarah, Plain and Tall

Extension: Have students write two sentences for a partner to combine into a sentence with a compound subject or predicate.

15

Punctuating Compound Sentences

- Use a comma before *and*, *but*, or *or* when you join two sentences to form a compound sentence.
- Begin every sentence with a capital letter.
- The second part of a compound sentence should not begin with a capital letter.

Correct each sentence. Write commas and capital letters where they are needed.

1. Papa gave Sarah daisies and she put them in her hair.

_____

2. the neighbors came to help and Maggie brought plants.

_____

3. the women planted flowers and the men plowed the fields.

_____

4. Sarah came by train and we went to meet her.

_____

5. the sky was dark green and the air was still.

_____

6. the work was done and the men came in from the field.

_____

7. Sarah will stay and there will be a wedding.

_____

8. Sarah brought candles and they ate by candlelight.

_____

Extension: Have pairs of students look through books and magazines to find examples of compound sentences. Have students copy one example and then rewrite it as two sentences.

McGraw-Hill School Division

Grade 4/Unit 1
Sarah, Plain and Tall
8

Sentence Combining

A. Add a comma and *and* to turn each pair of sentences into a compound sentence.

1. The wind howled. The dogs started to bark.

   _____

2. The rain stopped. The sun came out.

   _____

3. The whistle sounded. The train pulled into the station.

   _____

4. Nick sat beside Anna. Seal crawled into her lap.

   _____

B. Combine each pair of sentences by joining their subjects or predicates with *and*.

5. Anna wanted Sarah to stay. Caleb wanted Sarah stay.

   _____

6. Sarah took the wagon. Sarah went to town.

   _____

7. Old Bess pulled the wagon. Jack pulled the wagon.

   _____

8. Caleb sat on the porch. Caleb played with his moon snail shell.

   _____

Combining Sentences

> • A **compound sentence** contains two sentences joined by *and, but,* or *or.*
>
> • A **compound subject** contains two or more simple subjects that have the same predicate.
>
> • A **compound predicate** contains two or more simple predicates that have the same subject.

Mechanics

> • In a compound sentence, use a comma before *and, but,* or *or* when you join two sentences.
>
> • Begin every sentence with a capital letter.

Combine each pair of sentences to write one sentence that tells about the picture.

1. Amanda went for a walk. Bear went for a walk.

   _____

2. Bear pulled at the leash. Bear wouldn't heel.

   _____

Sentence Combining

A conjunction joins words, groups of words, or sentences.

> • You can use conjunctions other than *and, but,* or *or* to combine sentences.
>
> • Some conjunctions tell *where, when, why, how,* or *under what condition.*

Here is a list of some conjunctions:

where	when	why	how	although
as	before	because	as if	if
as soon as	after	since	as though	unless

Combine each pair of sentences using the conjunction given.

1. They traveled for hours. They reached the seal colony. (before)

_____

2. They could hear the baby seals. They stepped out on the ice. (as soon as)

_____

3. The mother seal knows her pup. She recognizes its scent. (because)

_____

4. Pups must learn to swim. They will spend their lives in the water. (since)

_____

5. He patted the whitecoat. He walked back to the helicopter. (before)

_____

6. Hunters couldn't sell seal fur. People wanted it. (unless)

_____

7. The hunters would have to stop. Nobody would buy the fur. (if)

_____

8. You could see the seal's markings. She nestled with her pup. (as)

_____

Extension: Have students find four compound sentences in the selection and identify the conjunction in each one.

Complex Sentences

> • A sentence that contains two related ideas joined by a conjunction other than *and, but,* or *or* is called a **complex sentence**.

Combine these ideas using the conjunction given to form a complex sentence.

1. The seals' swimming skills improve. They grow. (as)

_____

2. The mother and pup rub noses. The pup nurses. (while)

_____

3. Males keep their distance. Pups are being nursed. (while)

_____

4. The seals journey back north. They spend the summer. (where)

_____

5. They will return to the ice. Autumn comes. (when)

_____

6. Tourists want to see the whitecoats. That is what they came for. (since)

_____

7. The young pups feed on small shrimp. They swim along behind the herd. (as)

_____

8. Only twelve days pass. A seal pup is weaned. (before)

_____

9. The pup was still wet and yellow from its birth. They saw it. (when)

_____

10. We watched. The mother nudged the pup toward the water. (as)

_____

20

Extension: Have students write their own complex sentences using each of these conjunctions: *where, before,* and *because.*

Grade 4/Unit 1
Seal Journey 10

McGraw-Hill School Division

Combining Sentences

> • You can use conjunctions other than *and, but,* or *or* to combine sentences.
>
> • Some conjunctions tell *where, when, why, how,* or *under what condition.*
>
> • A sentence that contains two related ideas joined by a conjunction other than *and, but,* or *or* is called a **complex sentence**.

Combine these ideas using the conjunction given to form a complex sentence.

1. The frozen wilderness becomes a nursery. The seal pups are born. (when)

_____

2. The excitement started. The helicopter took off. (as soon as)

_____

3. Seals have to come up for air. They are mammals. (because)

_____

4. Mother and pup rubbed noses. They lay in the sun. (as)

_____

5. A seal pup is only twelve days old. It is weaned. (when)

_____

6. The male seal stays away. The pups are being born and nursed. (while)

_____

7. The male seals return. The pups are weaned. (once)

_____

8. The seal pups are no longer white. They join the herd. (when)

_____

Extension: Ask students to write three complex sentences about seals using these conjunctions: *whenever, although,* and *until.*

Quotations

> • Use quotation marks at the beginning and end of a person's exact words.
>
> • Do not use quotation marks when you do not use the speaker's exact words.

Add quotation marks where they are needed in these sentences.

1. He told us that he was going to Canada to photograph seals.

2. A large group of seals gathers there in winter, he explained.

3. He said Charlottetown would be his base camp.

4. He added, I leave for Prince Edward Island next week.

5. He said many people were making the journey these days.

6. He said it was a favorite destination for ecological tourists.

7. I don't consider myself an ecological tourist, he added.

8. He said, My interest is that of a serious scientist.

9. He admitted it would be his first visit to the icy world of the seal colony.

10. I do wonder how cold it actually gets, he said.

Extension: Ask students to write a sentence that includes a person's exact words. Have them give their sentences to a partner who will rewrite the sentence so that it tells what the person said but not in his or her exact words.

Grade 4/Unit 1
Seal Journey /10

Complex Sentences

Choose the best conjunction to combine each pair of sentences.

1. There were holes in the ice —————— the seals would dive into the water.

   a   until

   b   where

   c   unless

   d   before

2. They could hear the baby seals —————— they stepped out onto the ice.

   a   unless

   b   as though

   c   until

   d   as soon as

3. Seals must come up for air —————— they are mammals.

   a   if

   b   unless

   c   because

   d   although

4. The pup couldn't sink —————— he had so much fat.

   a   before

   b   although

   c   because

   d   as if

5. A mother must find her own pup —————— she only has enough milk for one.

   a   if

   b   since

   c   when

   d   unless

Sentence Combining and Quotations

> • You can use conjunctions other than *and, but,* or *or* to combine sentences.
>
> • A sentence that contains two related ideas joined by a conjunction other than *and, but,* or *or* is called a **complex sentence**.

Mechanics

> • Use quotation marks at the beginning and end of a person's exact words.
>
> • Do not use quotation marks when you do not use the speaker's exact words.

A. Combine each pair of ideas to form a complex sentence.

1. Jordan was sad. She read about hunters killing whitecoats.

_____

2. That horror is over now. People fought to end seal hunting.

_____

B. Look at the drawing above. Write what you think might be the boy's exact words. Write another sentence to tell what he says without using his exact words.

3. _____

_____

4. _____

_____

Run-on Sentences

> • A **run-on sentence** joins together two or more sentences that should be written separately.
>
> • You can correct a run-on sentence by separating two complete ideas into two sentences.

Read the run-on sentences below. Then correct them by separating them into two sentences.

1. Chimpanzees pull back their lips that's how they smile.

_____

2. Many zoos have dentists the dentists might have human patients, too.

_____

3. Pets need dental care most vets clean cats' and dogs' teeth regularly.

_____

4. Pet owners can do things to keep their pets' teeth clean they brush them.

_____

5. There is special toothpaste for dogs it tastes like beef.

_____

6. There are special biscuits and dog chews they keep teeth clean, too.

_____

7. Cats need to eat kibble it helps prevent tartar buildup.

_____

8. Dogs and cats use their sharp teeth to bite their flat teeth are for grinding.

_____

8

Grade 4/Unit 1
Open Wide, Don't Bite!

Extension: Have students write their own run-on sentence and give it to a partner to separate into two sentences.

25

Run-on Sentences

> • You can correct a run-on sentence by rewriting it as a compound or a complex sentence.

Correct these run-on sentences by rewriting them as compound or complex sentences.

1. The dog's teeth looked scary he was really smiling.

_____

2. An elephant would have a big toothache it has such big teeth.

_____

3. Large animals are good dental patients their mouths are so large.

_____

4. The dentist treats animals he has human patients, too.

_____

5. Carnivores have pointed teeth herbivores have flat teeth.

_____

6. A new tooth grows in an alligator loses a tooth.

_____

7. Beavers' teeth stay filed down they chew on wood.

_____

8. An animal can become sick it has a bad tooth.

_____

Extension: Have students write three run-on sentences to give to a partner who will rewrite them as compound or complex sentences.

Grade 4/Unit 1
Open Wide, Don't Bite!

8

Run-on Sentences

> - A **run-on sentence** joins together two or more sentences that should be written separately.
> - You can correct a run-on sentence by separating two complete ideas into two sentences.
> - You can correct a run-on sentence by rewriting it as a compound or complex sentence.

Read each sentence. If it is a run-on sentence, correct it by separating the two parts or rewrite it by adding a conjunction.

1. Some whales have teeth some have baleen instead.

_____

2. A sore tooth can hurt an animal a sore mouth can make an animal not

want to eat. _____

_____

3. It's hard to fix an aardvark's teeth their mouths don't open very far.

_____

4. Walruses have tusks tigers have fangs.

_____

5. Humans have teeth called canines they are pointed like dogs' teeth.

_____

6. Humans have sharp teeth and flat teeth so do dogs and cats.

_____

Extension: Ask students to write a compound or complex sentence on a strip of paper. Then have them cut the words apart and mix them up. Have them give their words to a partner who will arrange them first into two sentences and then into the original compound or complex sentence.

Sentence Punctuation

> • Every sentence begins with a capital letter.
>
> • Use the correct end mark for each sentence.

Add capital letters and punctuation to turn each set of words into a sentence.

1. a tiger's teeth are long and sharp

_____

2. the tiger relies on them for hunting

_____

3. elephants have big, flat teeth

_____

4. they are good for eating grasses and hay

_____

5. plant-eaters have flat teeth for chewing and grinding

_____

6. meat-eaters have long, pointed teeth for biting and tearing

_____

7. animals' teeth match their diet

_____

8. what do your teeth tell about your diet

_____

9. open wide _____

10. what big teeth you have

_____

28

Extension: Have pairs of students tape-record a brief conversation and then write down what they said, using capital letters and punctuation wherever needed.

Grade 4/Unit 1
Open Wide, Don't Bite! 10

Run-on Sentences

A. Correct these run-on sentences by separating them into two sentences.

1. A dentist was called to the zoo a tiger had a toothache.

_____

2. The tiger's face was swollen it would not eat.

_____

3. The dentist fixed the tooth he did not pull it.

_____

4. The tiger felt better he was hungry again.

_____

5. The dentist went back to his office human patients were waiting.

_____

B. Rewrite the following run-on sentences as compound or complex sentences.

6. The bear growled it had a toothache.

_____

7. It would grow weak the tooth could be fixed.

_____

8. The dentist went to the zoo he heard about it.

_____

9. The tooth had to come out it was infected.

_____

10. The bear lost a tooth it felt much better.

_____

Correcting Sentences

- A **run-on sentence** joins together two or more sentences that should be written separately.

- You can correct a run-on sentence by separating two complete ideas into two sentences.

- You can correct a run-on sentence by rewriting it as a compound or complex sentence.

Mechanics

- Begin every sentence with a capital letter.
- Use the correct end mark for each sentence.

Add capital letters and punctuation marks to turn each group of words into one or two sentences that tell about the picture above them.

1. mother hippo brought her baby the baby is getting a new tooth

_____

2. the dentist may need a ladder to treat the giraffe it is so tall

_____

3. the lion needs a filling he doesn't want it to show when he roars

_____

4. the crocodile wants braces his replacement teeth are coming in crooked

_____

5. the bear will growl the dentist sees him soon

_____

Sentences

Read each passage and look at the underlined sections. What kind of sentences are they? Circle your answers.

Luke and his dad set out to find their own lake. <u>Did they ever find it?</u> They
(1)

sure did. One morning they woke up and there it was. <u>What a surprise!</u>
(2)

1. A   Statement
    B   Question
    C   Command
    D   Exclamation

2. F   Statement
    G   Question
    H   Command
    J   Exclamation

The road seemed to whisper to Amelia, <u>"Follow me."</u> So she did. <u>She</u>
(3)

<u>discovered that it led to a big old tree.</u> She made that tree her own special
(4)

place, a place to come home to.

3. A   Statement
    B   Question
    C   Command
    D   Exclamation

4. F   Statement
    G   Question
    H   Command
    J   Exclamation

When Sarah went to town alone, the children were afraid she was leaving.

<u>They spent the whole day worrying.</u> It was almost dark when they heard the
(5)

wagon. <u>Sarah came back!</u>
(6)

5. A   Statement
    B   Question
    C   Command
    D   Exclamation

6. F   Statement
    G   Question
    H   Command
    J   Exclamation

Sentences

Read the passage and look at the underlined sentences. Is there a mistake? If there is, how do you correct it? Circle your answer.

> Baby seals used to be hunted for their beautiful white fur. <u>Those sweet baby seals with big dark eyes.</u> (7) People thought hunting them was terrible and cruel.
>
> <u>They worked to stop the hunting. They succeeded.</u> (8)

7. **A**   Add a subject.
   B   Add a predicate.
   C   Join two sentences with *and.*
   D   No mistake.

8. **F**   Add a subject.
   G   Add a predicate.
   H   Join two sentences with *and.*
   J   No mistake.

> Humans share lots of things with animals. <u>Might share a dentist.</u> (9) <u>There are dentists who have human patients. They have animal patients, too.</u> (10)

9. **A**   Add a subject.
   B   Add a predicate.
   C   Join two sentences with *and.*
   D   No mistake.

10. **F**   Add a subject.
    G   Add a predicate.
    H   Join two sentences with *and.*
    J   No mistake.

Common and Proper Nouns

> • A **noun names** a person, place, or thing.
>
> • A **common noun** names any person, place, or thing.
>
> • A **proper noun** names a particular person, place, or thing.
>
> • A proper noun begins with a capital letter.

Underline the common nouns in each sentence. Then double underline the proper nouns in each sentence.

1. Justin and Grandpa rode horses across the meadow.

2. Grandpa rode Pal, and Justin rode Black.

3. Justin and Grandpa checked the fence for broken places.

4. Suddenly, the boy saw a fawn caught in the wire.

5. Grandpa mixed dough and cooked delicious biscuits.

6. Justin learned that both men and women can be cooks.

7. The cardinal made a sound like a whistle.

8. Anthony had a dog named Pepper.

Grade 4/Unit 2
Justin and the Best Biscuits in the World

Extension: Ask students to write two sentences about the story using both common and proper nouns. Have partners exchange papers and draw a line under the nouns in each other's sentences.

33

Proper Nouns

> • Some proper nouns contain more than one word. Each important word begins with a capital letter.
>
> • The name of a day, month, or holiday begins with a capital letter.

Capitalize the proper nouns found in each sentence.

1. The rodeo sport bulldogging was invented by bill pickett.

   _____

2. He lived on a ranch in the state of oklahoma. _____

3. Some states have cold weather in january. _____

4. People think jessie stahl rode wild horses better than anyone.

   _____

5. The comedian will rogers was taught how to rope by a cowboy.

   _____

6. This cowboy was known as clay. _____

7. Another famous cowboy had the nickname deadwood dick.

   _____

8. He got his name from the town of deadwood city.

   _____

Extension: Invite small groups of students to write sentences describing the Black cowboys mentioned in the story. Remind students to capitalize proper nouns.

Grade 4/Unit 2
Justin and the Best Biscuits in the World   8

Common and Proper Nouns

- A **noun** names a person, place, or thing.

- A **common noun** names any person, place, or thing.

- A **proper noun** names a particular person, place, or thing.

- Some proper nouns contain more than one word. Each important word begins with a capital letter.

- The name of a day, month, or holiday begins with a capital letter.

Write a common noun or proper noun to complete each sentence. For help you may look back at the story.

1. Grandpa showed ———————— how to fold a shirt.

2. Grandpa's ———————— were named Cropper, Pal, and Black.

3. Justin's grandpa lived on a ————————.

4. Justin thought of Anthony, his ———————— back home.

5. The baby ———————— got caught on the fence.

6. Deadwood ————————'s real name was Nate Love.

7. Justin told Grandpa that housework was women's ————————.

8. Instead of chores, Justin wanted to play ball on Saturday and ————————.

Extension: Have students write a paragraph that describes one of the characters from the story. After they have finished, ask students to underline the common nouns and circle the proper nouns in their writing.

Abbreviations

- An **abbreviation** is the shortened form of a word.

- An abbreviation begins with a capital letter and ends with a period.

- Abbreviate titles of people before names.

- You can abbreviate days of the week. You can also abbreviate most months.

Write each abbreviation correctly.

A Rancher's Calendar:

1. July -- Look for picture of mr Pickett. _____

2. aug -- Grandson comes to visit. _____

3. mon -- Ride fence. _____

4. wed -- Have dr Jones look at sick cow. _____

5. thurs -- Buy gift for mrs Friend. _____

6. sat -- Judge festival. _____

7. nov -- Buy hay for winter. _____

8. dec -- Drop hay bales for cattle. _____

Extension: Have students look for abbreviations in newspapers and magazines and circle the ones they find.

Grade 4/Unit 2
Justin and the Best Biscuits in the World

8

Common and Proper Nouns

Find two nouns in each sentence and write them on the lines.

1. The nervous doe watched Grandpa carefully. _____

2. A few clouds floated over the foothills. _____

3. Black drank at the stream first. _____

4. Deadwood City was in the Dakota Territory. _____

Use the nouns in the box to complete each sentence in a way that makes sense. Don't forget to capitalize any proper nouns.

| justin | plain | snake | teddy roosevelt |

5. After racing across the _____ Black was calm.

6. Justin thought a _____ might be in the grass.

7. Grandpa told _____ about Black cowboys.

8. One Black cowboy helped _____.

Common and Proper Nouns

- A **common noun** names any person, place, or thing.

- A **proper noun** names a particular person, place, or thing.

Mechanics:

- Begin each important word in a proper noun with a capital letter.

- Begin the name of a day, month, or holiday with a capital letter.

Read each sentence. Write the underlined noun correctly on the line.

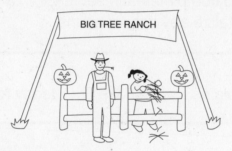

1. The <u>Rancher</u> is wearing a cowboy hat. _____

2. He carved two pumpkins for <u>halloween</u> and put them on posts.

   _____

3. The name of the ranch, <u>big tree ranch</u>, is on a sign.

   _____

4. The girl is dropping <u>Hay</u> over the fence. _____

Singular and Plural Nouns

- A **singular noun** names one person, place, or thing.

- A **plural noun** names more than one person, place, or thing.

- Add -*s* to form the plural of most singular nouns.

Decide whether each underlined word is a singular or plural noun. Then write an "S" for singular or a "P" for plural on the line.

1. There were three trash <u>cans</u> in the garage. —————

2. One can had only <u>bottles</u> in it. —————

3. Walter traveled to the future in his <u>bed</u>. —————

4. Walter did not like the <u>dream</u> he had. —————

5. He put his head under the <u>blankets</u>. —————

6. Smoke poured from the <u>smokestack</u> by Walter's bed. —————

7. <u>Trucks</u> honked loudly all around the bed. —————

8. A woman showed Walter <u>postcards</u> of the Grand Canyon. —————

9. A <u>duck</u> that could talk landed on Walter's bed. —————

10. Walter was glad to get back to his <u>room</u>. —————

10 Grade 4/Unit 2
Just a Dream

Extension: Have students make a list of the underlined singular nouns. Then ask students to add -*s* to each word and write its plural form.

39

Forming Plural Nouns

- Add *-es* to form the plural of singular nouns that end in *s*, *sh*, *ch*, or *x*.

- To form the plural of nouns ending in a consonant and *y*, change *y* to *i* and add *-es*.

- To form the plural of nouns ending in a vowel and *y*, add *-s*.

Find the plural noun in the box for each underlined singular noun in the sentences below. Write the plural noun on the line.

gases	wishes	branches	boxes
bakeries	parties	toys	highways

1. Doughnuts and other sweets are made in <u>bakery</u> ——————.

2. There were <u>box</u> —————— of trash in the huge dump.

3. Walter's bed landed on <u>branch</u> —————— in a tree.

4. Deadly <u>gas</u> —————— filled the air.

5. The <u>highway</u> —————— in the future were crowded.

6. Walter's birthday <u>wish</u> —————— all came true.

7. He got many new <u>toy</u> —————— and a tree.

8. Of all his birthday <u>party</u> —————— he liked this one best.

Extension: Have students make a Singular and Plural chart. Ask students to list singular nouns ending in *s*, *sh*, *ch*, *x*, and *y* and then write the plurals of these words.

McGraw-Hill School Division

Forming Plural Nouns

- Add -s to form the plural of most singular nouns.

- Add -es to form the plural of singular nouns that end in s, sh, ch, or x.

- To form the plural of nouns ending in a consonant and y, change y to i and add -es.

- To form the plural of nouns ending in a vowel and y, add -s.

Write the correct plural form of each noun in parentheses.

1. Walter's street was filled with (boxs) —————— and bags of trash.

2. Two (woodcutteries) ————————— cut down a tall tree.

3. In the mountains, Walter saw people wearing (snowshoe) —————.

4. All around Walter, cars and (busies) ————— were honking.

5. The traffic moved slowly, only (inchs) ————— at a time.

6. Walter thought there would be robots in the (citys) ————.

7. Walter felt peaceful outside next to the trees and (bushs) ————.

8. He enjoyed the blue sky and warm (ray) ————— from the sun.

McGraw-Hill School Division

Extension: Have students brainstorm ideas about the future. Ask them to make a list of singular nouns that name a person, place, or thing of the future. Then have students write the plural form of each singular noun.

41

Commas in a Series

> - A **comma** tells the reader to pause between the words that it separates.
>
> - Use commas to separate three or more words in a series.
>
> - Do not use a comma after the last word in a series.

Add commas where they belong in each sentence.

1. An airplane robot and machine were on the TV show Walter watched.

   _____

2. There were trash cans for bottles cans and garbage.

   _____

3. Trash traffic smoke and dirt were in Walter's dream.

   _____

4. Walter now wants clean air land and water in his future.

   _____

5. A dinosaur yo-yo and tree were Walter's birthday presents.

   _____

6. Some day squirrels bugs and birds may live in Walter's tree.

   _____

Extension: Ask pairs of students to write two sentences, using three or more words in a series, leaving out the commas. Then have partners exchange papers and add missing commas to each other's sentences.

McGraw-Hill School Division

Singular and Plural Nouns

Read each sentence. Find the noun that is singular. Circle your answer.

1. The medicine was to help sore throats and itchy eyes.

   a. medicine   **b.** throats   **c.** itchy   **d.** eyes

2. Snowflakes fell as the hikers climbed up to the hotel.

   a. snowflakes   **b.** fell   **c.** hikers   **d.** hotel

3. There were stars and ducks in the black sky.

   a. stars   **b.** ducks   **c.** black   **d.** sky

4. A gentle breeze blew the leaves on two tall trees.

   a. gentle   **b.** breeze   **c.** leaves   **d.** trees

Read each sentence. Find the correct plural form for the noun in parentheses.

5. The (sky) in Walter's dream were filled with smoke or snow or smog.

   a. skys   **b.** skyes   **c.** skies   **d.** skyies

6. Both Walter and Rose planted trees on their (birthday).

   a. birthdays   **b.** birthdayes   **c.** birthdaies   **d.** birthdayies

7. Walter's friends had slices of cake and (dish) of ice cream.

   a. dishs   **b.** dishes   **c.** dishies   **d.** dishyes

8. Walter never saw so many (pastry) on one plate before.

   a. pastrys   **b.** pastres   **c.** pastrees   **d.** pastries

Singular and Plural Nouns

- Add -s to form the plural of most singular nouns.
- Add -es to form the plural of singular nouns that end in s, sh, ch, or x.
- To form the plural of nouns ending in a consonant and y, change y to i and add -es.
- To form the plural of nouns ending in a vowel and y, add -s.

Mechanics:

- A comma tells the reader to pause between the words that it separates.
- Use commas to separate three or more words in a series.
- Do not use a comma after the last word in a series.

Correct each sentence below by changing the underlined singular noun to a plural, and by adding the missing commas. With a partner, take turns reading the corrected sentences aloud, pausing when you reach each comma.

1. Walter saw trash covering <u>house</u> streets and trees.

_____

2. Smoke from <u>factory</u> hurt his eyes nose and throat.

_____

3. The only <u>animal</u> Walter saw were a horse a fish and ducks.

_____

4. Now Walter likes to sort <u>can</u> bottles and <u>box</u>.

_____

Irregular Plural Nouns

> • Some nouns have special plural forms.

calves	children	feet	geese	gentlemen
lives	men	oxen	teeth	women

Look in the above box for the plural form of each singular noun. Write it on the line provided.

1. man ——————

2. child ——————

3. woman ——————

4. life ——————

5. calf ——————

6. goose ——————

7. ox ——————

8. foot ——————

9. tooth ——————

10. gentleman ——————

10 Grade 4/Unit 2
Leah's Pony

Extension: Have partners take turns using the singular and plural nouns on this page in oral sentences.

45

Irregular Plural Nouns

- A few nouns have the same singular and plural forms.

Read the sentences below. Then decide whether the underlined word is a singular noun or plural noun and write singular or plural on the line.

1. There was not one <u>sheep</u> on Papa's farm. —————

2. There was no grass in his dry field for <u>sheep</u> to eat. —————

3. Some farms have ponds with <u>fish</u> in them. —————

4. Have you ever seen a <u>fish</u> in a pond? —————

5. Farmers in Maine may see a <u>moose</u> drink from a pond. —————

6. <u>Moose</u> are much bigger animals than cows. —————

7. Moose and <u>deer</u> are not farm animals. —————

8. A <u>deer</u> could jump over a farmer's fence. —————

Extension: Ask students to draw pictures illustrating the singular and plural forms of the words *sheep*, *fish*, *moose*, and *deer*. Have students write captions for their pictures.

Grade 4/Unit 2
Leah's Pony
8

McGraw-Hill School Division

Plural Nouns

- Some nouns have special plural forms.
- A few nouns have the same singular and plural forms.

Read each sentence. Draw a line under the word in parentheses that is the correct plural form.

1. Of all the (ponys, ponies) in the county, Leah's pony was the finest.

2. Leah waved to the (childs, children) in the truck.

3. (Boxes, Boxs) full of the family's things were piled into the truck.

4. The (lifes, lives) of farmers were hard in these times.

5. The land was too dry for farm animals like (sheep, sheeps) and cattle.

6. There were no (fishes, fish) because the streams had dried up.

7. Several (men, mans) came to the auction.

8. Sometimes (calfs, calves) were sold at an auction.

9. A man in a big hat called out, "Ladies and (gentlemans, gentlemen)."

10. A farmer gave Papa the (keys, keyes) to the truck.

---

10 Grade 4/Unit 2
   Leah's Pony

Extension: Have students name the two nouns in the above sentences that have the same singular and plural forms. Then ask students to name the five nouns that have special plural forms.

47

Capitalization

> - A proper noun begins with a capital letter.
> - The name of a day, month, or holiday begins with a capital letter.
> - Capitalize family names if they refer to specific people.
> - Capitalize titles of people before names.

Read the sentences below. Then correct the capitalization mistakes and rewrite the sentences on the line provided.

1. When leah went into town, she always rode by the grocery store.

_____

2. She knew mr. b. liked to see her pony.

_____

3. Leah's mother always baked coffee cake on saturday.

_____

4. One day, the neighbors moved to oregon.

_____

5. Because times were hard, papa had to sell his tractor.

_____

6. Papa's tractor was made by a company named farmall.

_____

7. The family also had to sell mama's prize rooster.

_____

8. The story about leah and her pony was written by elizabeth friedrich.

_____

Extension: Ask students to write four sentences that have words beginning with capital letters. The sentences must include the following kinds of names: a month, a holiday, a person's name, and a person's name with a title.

Grade 4/Unit 2
Leah's Pony
8

Irregular Plural Nouns

A. Write *yes* if the noun below has the same singular and plural forms.
Write *no* if the noun does not have the same singular and plural forms.

1. rooster ——————

2. deer ——————

3. sheep ——————

4. pony ——————

5. moose ——————

6. calf ——————

B. Complete each sentence with the plural form of the singular noun in
parentheses.

7. Leah's (foot) —————— were dusty because she walked home.

8. It was hard for (woman) —————— to keep the houses clean.

9. Most (child) —————— on a farm have chores to do.

10. Even the (mouse) —————— that lived in the fields had little to eat.

Irregular Plural Nouns

- Some nouns have special plural forms.
- A few nouns have the same singular and plural forms.

Mechanics

- A proper noun begins with a capital letter.
- The name of a day, month, or holiday begins with a capital letter.
- Capitalize family names if they refer to specific people.
- Capitalize titles of people before names.

Read the sentences and correct any underlined plural noun. Include any word or words that need to be capitalized on the line provided.

1. The author of <u>storys</u> about leah lives on a farm in new hampshire.

_____

2. She has a horse and six <u>sheeps</u> on her farm.

_____

3. When she was young, ms. friedrich liked to visit a farm in missouri.

_____

4. In a farm family, men, <u>womans</u>, and <u>childs</u> help with the work.

_____

5. Farmers work on weekdays and also on saturday and Sunday.

_____

Possessive Nouns

- A **possessive noun** is a noun that shows who or what owns or has something.

- A **singular possessive noun** is a singular noun that shows ownership.

- Form a singular possessive noun by adding an **apostrophe (')** and an *-s* to a singular noun.

Write the possessive form of each underlined singular noun.

1. The <u>boy</u> family had to live in a camp. _____

2. Many of the <u>family</u> things had to be thrown away. _____

3. A soldier watched everyone from the <u>Camp</u> tower. _____

4. The older men were surprised at <u>Teddy</u> words. _____

5. Would <u>Dad</u> idea for a baseball field work? _____

6. Each <u>team</u> uniforms were made from mattress covers. _____

7. In the ninth inning, the <u>game</u> score was 3 to 2. _____

8. The boy heard the <u>catcher</u> voice. _____

9. He saw the gleam of the <u>guard</u> sunglasses. _____

10. The ball sailed over the left <u>fielder</u> _____ head.

Extension: Have students write four sentences, using four of the singular possessive nouns from these sentences. The sentences do not have to be about the story. As students share their sentences, have them check the placement of apostrophes.

Plural Possessive Nouns

* A **plural possessive noun** is a plural noun that shows ownership.

* To form the possessive of a plural noun that ends in *s*, add an apostrophe.

* To form the possessive of a plural noun that does not end in s, add an apostrophe and an *-s*.

Write the possessive form of each underlined plural noun. Add an apostrophe or an apostrophe and *-s*.

1. In Camp, the <u>babies</u> cries kept people awake. —————

2. The <u>soldiers</u> job was to watch everyone. —————

3. The sound of the <u>women</u> sewing machines filled the room. —————

4. The <u>men</u> work was building the bleachers. —————

5. Soon the <u>families</u> children helped pack down the dust. —————

6. There were bats, balls, and gloves in the <u>friends</u> sacks. —————

7. The <u>kids</u> teams played all the time. —————

8. After his home run, the boy rode on his <u>teammates</u> shoulders. —————

Extension: Ask students to write sentences from the story. Have them use the possessive forms of these plural nouns: *players, parents, children, teams.*

Grade 4/Unit 2
Baseball Saved Us
8

McGraw-Hill School Division

Singular and Plural Possessive Nouns

- A **possessive noun** is a noun that shows who or what owns or has something.

- A **singular possessive noun** is a singular noun that shows ownership.

- A **plural possessive noun** is a plural noun that shows ownership.

Read these sentences. Draw one line under each singular possessive noun. Draw two lines under each plural possessive noun.

1. One day the boy's parents came to his school.

2. Both parents' faces were very sad.

3. In Camp, most of the older boys' time was spent standing around.

4. Teddy's dad asked him to get some water.

5. At first, the field's dirt was dry and cracked.

6. All of the kids' sizes were about the same.

7. Did the man's staring bother the boy?

8. At home, the players' nickname for the boy was Shorty.

Extension: As a class, brainstorm for a list of singular nouns that could show possession. Then arrange students into two teams. In spelling-bee format, have teams challenge each other to form the singular and plural possessive forms of the nouns.

Apostrophes

- Add an apostrophe and an *-s* to a singular noun to make it possessive.

- Add an apostrophe to make most plural nouns possessive.

- Add an apostrophe and an *-s* to form the possessive of plural nouns that do not end in *s.*

Read the first sentence in each pair. Use the possessive form of the underlined noun to complete the second sentence.

1. The players thought of a name for their baseball <u>team</u>.

The——————— name is the Mighty Moose.

2. It's easy to tell which kids play for the <u>Moose</u>.

All the ——————— caps have antlers on them.

3. What color did the <u>players</u> choose for their uniforms?

The ——————— uniforms are brown.

4. What a good <u>pitcher</u> the team has!

The ——————— fast ball is great.

5. The Mighty Moose have many <u>fans</u>.

You will see antlers on some of the ——————— heads.

Extension: Have students work in pairs. One student lists five nouns; the other writes their possessive forms. Have students reverse their tasks.

Grade 4/Unit 2
Baseball Saved Us

5

TEST

Singular and Plural Possessive Nouns

Choose the correct singular possessive form to complete each sentence.

1. The ——————— eyes were watching me play ball.

   a. soldier'   **b.** soldiers'   **c.** soldiers   **d.** soldier's

2. The ——————— glove was brown.

   a. fielders'   **b.** fielder's   **c.** fielders's   **d.** fielder'

3. The ——————— bat was lying on the ground.

   a. boy's   **b.** boy   **c.** boys'   **d.** boys's

4. The ——————— baseball field needed to be cleaned up.

   a. Camps'   **b.** Camp's   **c.** Camps's   **d.** Camps

Choose the correct plural possessive form to complete each sentence.

5. The ——————— parents were sad about moving.

   a. brothers'   **b.** brothers   **c.** brother's   **d.** brother'

6. The ——————— bats came from friends back home.

   a. player'   **b.** player's   **c.** players'   **d.** players's

7. The ——————— games were fun to watch.

   a. children'   **b.** children's   **c.** children   **d.** childrens'

8. Our ——————— help is needed to make our lives better.

   a. parents'   **b.** parent   **c.** parents   **d.** parent'

Singular and Plural Possessive Nouns

- A **singular possessive noun** is a singular noun that shows ownership.

- A **plural possessive noun** is a plural noun that shows ownership.

Mechanics:

- Add an apostrophe and an -s to a singular noun to make it possessive.

- Add an apostrophe to make most plural nouns possessive.

- Add an apostrophe and an -s to form the possessive of plural nouns that do not end in s.

Work with a partner. Read the sentences aloud. Then make each underlined noun possessive. Be sure to write the possessive forms correctly.

1. <u>Dad</u> mark was the beginning of a baseball field. _____

2. Soon both <u>players</u> baseball equipment arrived. _____

3. The other <u>team</u> players made jokes. _____

4. The Camp had a new activity because of many <u>people</u> hard work.

_____

5. Did the <u>boy</u> hit win the game? _____

Plural and Possessive Nouns

> • A **plural noun** names more than one person, place, or thing.
>
> • Add *-s* to most nouns to form the plural. Do not use an apostrophe.

Write the plural form of the noun in parentheses on the line provided.

1. Sealy could not speak to his (classmate) _____ in English.

2. None of the (kid) _____ knew the Choctaw language.

3. About 12,000 (person) _____ speak Choctaw.

4. Many (language) _____ are endangered.

5. Some (book) _____ are now being printed in Choctaw.

6. There are (recording) _____ in the Choctaw language.

7. Native American (child) _____ forgot their native languages.

8. Older (relative) _____ don't know English.

9. Picture writing was used to record family (history) _____.

10. Can you say some (word) _____ in Choctaw?

10 Grade 4/Unit 2
Will Her Native Language Disappear?

Extension: Have pairs of students find five other singular nouns in the story *Will Her Native Language Disappear?* Ask partners to list these nouns and then write the plural form of each one.

57

Possessive Nouns

> • A **possessive noun** shows who or what owns or has something.
>
> • Add an apostrophe and -*s* to a singular noun to make it possessive.

Write the possessive form of each singular noun in parentheses.

1. A young (boy) ——————— only language was Choctaw.

2. In school, the (teacher) ————— language was English.

3. One group of people start to speak another (group) ————— language.

4. Many of the (world) ————— languages could disappear.

5. LeRoy (Sealy) ————— goal is to keep Choctaw from disappearing.

6. This Native (American) ————— home is in Oklahoma.

7. Today the (man) ————— niece is learning Choctaw.

8. A (turtle) ————— name in Choctaw is *loksi*.

Extension: Encourage students to write their own sentences, using the possessive forms of the nouns in parentheses in sentences 1-4.

Grade 4/Unit 2
Will Her Native Language Disappear?

/8

Plural and Possessive Nouns

- A **plural noun** names more than one person, place, or thing.
- Add -s to most nouns to form the plural. Do not use an apostrophe.
- A **possessive noun** shows who or what owns or has something.
- Add an apostrophe and -s to a singular noun to make it possessive.

Write a plural noun or a possessive noun to complete each sentence. Use the singular nouns in the box below to help you.

| arrow | book | computer | group | kid | picture | tribe | word |

1. Two common Choctaw _____ are *jkana* and *halito*.

2. One _____ meaning is "friend."

3. Pictures on rocks and hides told a _____ history.

4. Native Americans drew _____ to record events.

5. Sometimes they drew _____ to show directions.

6. An _____ tip might point up or down.

7. Some Native American _____ forgot their native language.

8. A group prints _____ in endangered languages.

9. This _____ name is the Endangered Language Fund.

10. Machines like _____ have spread English around the world.

Extension: Have students work in pairs. Ask each student to write two sentences, one with any plural noun and one with any possessive noun. Then have students trade papers and identify the plural noun and possessive noun in their partner's sentences.

Plural and Possessive Nouns

- Add -s to most nouns to form the plural. Do not use an apostrophe.

- Add an apostrophe and -s to a singular noun to make it possessive.

Add an -s or an apostrophe and an -s to the underlined word in each sentence. Use the line provided for your answer.

1. Can you speak two <u>language</u>? _____

2. Is English your <u>family</u> native language? _____

3. LeRoy <u>Sealy</u> native language is Choctaw. _____

4. Years ago, Native American children went to government <u>school</u>. _____

5. The <u>kid</u> spoke English and not their Native American language. _____

6. Usually a <u>child</u> parents did not know how to speak English. _____

7. Sealy teaches Choctaw to <u>student</u> in Oklahoma. _____

8. The <u>teacher</u> great worry is that the Choctaw language will disappear.

   _____

Extension: Ask each student to write a plural noun and a possessive noun on separate slips of paper. Put the slips in a box and invite students to take turns picking a slip. Have students tell how they know whether the word they picked is a plural or a possessive.

Grade 4/Unit 2
Will Her Native Language Disappear?

8

Plurals and Possessives

A. Decide whether each underlined word is a plural noun or a possessive noun. Then write plural or possessive on the line provided.

1. LeRoy Sealy had some lonely <u>days</u> in school. ———————

2. The <u>boy's</u> problem was that he could not communicate. ——————

3. The <u>man's</u> niece is named Patricia. ——————

4. Sealy uses <u>pictures</u> to teach his niece Choctaw. ——————

B. Choose the plural noun or possessive noun that best completes each sentence. Write it on the line provided.

5. Picture writing was one way that (tribes, tribe's) communicated. ——————

6. The many (tribes, tribe's) spoke different languages. ——————

7. Picture writing told a (tribes, tribe's) history. ——————

8. Some pictures told about important (events, event's). ——————

Plural and Possessive Nouns

- A plural noun names more than one person, place, or thing.
- A possessive noun shows who or what owns or has something.

Mechanics:

- Add -*s* to most nouns to form the plural. Do not use an apostrophe.
- Add an apostrophe and -*s* to a singular noun to make it possessive.

Read the sentences about the picture below. Then find the plural and possessive nouns that are not written correctly. Rewrite the sentences on the lines below, correcting the plural or possessive nouns.

1. What does this pages picture show you?

_____

2. Where are the two horse going?

_____

3. There is no saddle on either horse' back.

_____

4. This picture shows rain falling on the mountains top.

_____

Nouns

Read each passage. Choose a word or group of words that belong in each space. Circle your answer.

When Justin visited ——————— grandfather, he learned about some famous

                 (1)

cowboys. One cowboy was ——————. Many people thought he rode

                    (2)

wild horses better than anyone else. Justin said that he had never heard of

Mr. Stahl.

---

1. **A**   him
   B   he's
   C   his
   D   her

2. **F**   Mister Jessie stahl
   G   Mr. Jessie Stahl
   H   Mr Jessie Stahl
   J   Mr. jessie stahl

Walter had a dream about the future. In one part of his dream, his bed was

sitting in the ——————— of a tree. Then he was on a factory's smokestack. The

          (3)

smoke from the ——————— hurt his eyes, nose, and throat.

            (4)

---

3. **A**   branch's
   B   branchs
   C   branches
   D   branchese

4. **F**   ace medicine factory
   G   Ace Medicine Factory
   H   Ace medicine factory
   J   Ace Medicine factory

Nouns

Leah's father had to sell his ——————— at an auction. Leah sold her
(5)

pony and bought the tractor. Some farmers at the auction bought the

chickens and truck. Then ——————— gave them back to the family.
(6)

5. **A** chickens, Ford pickup
       truck, and tractor

   B chickens ford pickup truck
       and tractor

   C chicken's, Ford pickup
       truck, and tractor

   D chickens Ford pickup
       truck, and tractor

6. **F** these Men

   G the man's

   H the men

   J the mens'

Dad decided the Camp needed a baseball field. Grown-ups and kids

helped make the field. The ———————, made of mattress covers, looked good.
(7)

When the boy hit his home run, he looked up and saw the ———————.
(8)

7. **A** players' uniforms
   B players' uniform's
   C players uniform's
   D player's uniform

8. **F** guards thumb's-up sign
   G guards' thumbs'-up sign
   H guard's thumbs-up sign
   J guard thumb-up sign

Many ——————— do not know their native language. They speak only English.
(9)

LeRoy Sealy's native language is Choctaw. He teaches Choctaw to

students at the University of Oklahoma. Sealy worries that the ———————
(10)

——————— will disappear.

9. **A** Native Americans
   B Native American's
   C native americans
   D Native's Americans

10. **F** worlds languages
   G worlds' languages'
   H world language
   J world's languages

Grade 4/Unit 2
Something In Common /10

Action Verbs in the Present Tense

- An **action verb** tells what the subject does or did.

- A verb in the **present tense** tells what happens now.

- The present tense must have **subject-verb agreement**. Add *-s* to most verbs if the subject is singular. Do not add *-s* if the subject is plural or *I* or *you*.

Write the correct present tense of each underlined verb on the lines provided.

1. John Thompson <u>place</u> hats in the window of his shop. ——————

2. He <u>stack</u> hatboxes along a wall. ——————

3. John <u>write</u> some words on parchment. ——————

4. He <u>draw</u> a picture of a hat under the words. ——————

5. John <u>show</u> his idea for a sign to his wife. ——————

6. His wife giggles when she <u>read</u> the words. ——————

7. John <u>make</u> changes in his sign. ——————

8. The hatmaker <u>walk</u> to the sign maker's shop. ——————

9. The hatmaker <u>meet</u> many people on the way. ——————

10. What does the sign maker <u>say</u> to the hat maker? ——————

Extension: Have students write three sentences about the story, using the present tense of these verbs: *grab, rewrite, suggest*. Ask students to circle the verbs in their sentences.

Action Verbs

- Add *-es* to verbs that end in *s, ch, sh, x,* or *z* if the subject is singular.

- Change *y* to *i* and add *-es* to verbs that end with a consonant and *y*.

- Do not add *-es* to a present-tense verb when the subject is plural or *I* or *you*.

Read each sentence. Write the correct present tense of each underlined verb on the line provided.

1. Thomas Jefferson is angry, and his face <u>flush</u> red. ——————————

2. Benjamin Franklin <u>try</u> to make Jefferson feel better. ——————————

3. The hatmaker <u>kiss</u> Lady Manderly's hand. ——————————

4. The lady <u>snatch</u> the parchment away from the hatmaker.

   ——————————

5. John Thompson <u>toss</u> coins to the boys. ——————————

6. He <u>push</u> the parchment under a man's nose. ——————————

7. John <u>hurry</u> home to his shop several times. ——————————

8. The hatmaker <u>fix</u> the words on his sign. ——————————

9. John <u>rush</u> to the sign maker's shop. ——————————

10. Do you <u>realize</u> what happens to the hatmaker's sign?

    ——————————

Extension: Ask students to write five sentences, using these verbs: watch, watches; worry, worries.

Grade 4/Unit 3
The Hatmaker's Sign 10

McGraw-Hill School Division

Write Subject-Verb Agreement

- The present tense must have **subject-verb agreement**. Add *-s* to most verbs if the subject is singular.

- Add *-es* to verbs that end in *s, ch, sh, x,* or *z* if the subject is singular.

- Change *y* to *i* and add *-es* to verbs that end with a consonant and *y*.

- Do not add *-s* or *-es* to a present-tense verb when the subject is plural or *I* or *you*.

Correct each sentence for subject-verb agreement or the correct spelling of a present tense verb. Write your answer on the line provided.

1. Jefferson write for hours. ——————————

2. Many men listens to Jefferson read. ——————————

3. They argues about Jefferson's words. ——————————

4. Jefferson wishs they would stop quibbling. ——————————

5. He worrys about his writing. ——————————

6. Franklin pat Jefferson on the shoulder. ——————————

7. John carrys the parchment to the sign maker's shop. ——————————

8. Do you likes the story about the hatmaker? ——————————

8

Grade 4/Unit 3
The Hatmaker's Sign

Extension: Have students look in classroom books for sentences with present-tense verbs. Then have the students read the sentences aloud, identify the verbs, and tell whether the subject is singular or plural.

67

Commas in a Series

- A **comma** tells the reader to pause between the words that it separates.
- Use commas to separate three or more words in a series.
- Do not use a comma after the last word in a series.

Rewrite the sentences below by adding commas where they belong.

1. A good writer thinks writes and rewrites.

_____

2. The delegates shouted quibbled and argued over sentences.

_____

3. Benjamin Franklin stood smiled and spoke to Jefferson.

_____

4. Then Benjamin Franklin Jefferson's friend told a story.

_____

5. John Thompson a hatmaker wanted a sign for his shop.

_____

6. John's shop was in Boston Massachusetts.

_____

7. John's wife Hannah thought his sign was funny.

_____

8. Under the words on his sign John drew a hat.

_____

9. John rewrote rewrote and rewrote his sign.

_____

10. Surprised the sign maker gazed at the blank parchment.

_____

Extension: Ask students to write three sentences, using commas. Then tell students to rewrite the sentences without the commas. Have students exchange papers and put the missing commas in classmates' sentences.

Grade 4/Unit 3
The Hatmaker's Sign
10

Action Verbs in the Present Tense

A. Read each sentence. Circle the letter of the sentence that has correct subject-verb agreement.

1. **a.** Jefferson sit down.

   b. He listen carefully.

   c. Franklin tells a story.

   d. The delegates talks loudly.

2. **a.** The man draw a hat.

   b. His wife giggles.

   c. The lady wear gloves.

   d. John bow to the magistrate.

B. Read each sentence. Circle the letter before the present-tense verb that belongs in the sentence. Make sure the spelling is correct.

3. Jefferson _____ the meaning of Franklin's story.

   a. know

   b. knows

   c. knowes

   d. knowies

4. The wind _____ the hatmaker's sign from his hand.

   a. snatch

   b. snatchs

   c. snatches

   d. snatchies

Present Tense

- The present tense must have subject-verb agreement.
- Add *-s* to most verbs if the subject is singular.
- Add *-es* to verbs that end in *s, ch, sh, x,* or *z* if the subject is singular.
- Change *y* to *i* and add *-es* to verbs that end with a consonant and *y*.

Mechanics

- A comma tells the reader to pause between words that it separates.
- Use commas to separate three or more words in a series.
- Do not use a comma after the last word in a series.

Rewrite each sentence correctly paying attention to the present tense verb and comma rules. Then use the information in the sentences to draw the missing parts of the picture.

1. A hatmaker James hang a sign on his shop's door.

_____

2. George a clerk polishs a round mirror.

_____

3. One man sit and try on a top hat.

_____

4. Two ladies likes hats with bows ribbons and feathers.

_____

Past Tense

- A verb in the past tense tells about an action that already happened.

- Add -ed to most verbs to show past tense.

- If a verb ends with e, drop the e and add -ed.

- If a verb ends with a consonant and y, change y to i and add -ed.

- If a verb ends with one vowel and one consonant, double the consonant and add -ed.

Choose a verb for each sentence. Write the verb in the past tense.

1. When she was little, Pat Cummings _____ on a bus. (hop, help)

2. The bus _____ at a ballet school. (stop, walk)

3. Pat _____ with the girls in the class. (dance, shout)

4. Pat's mother _____ about her little girl. (hurry, worry)

5. She _____ everywhere for Pat. (jump, look)

6. When she was a child, Pat _____ to draw. (love, talk)

7. She _____ all over a sheet of paper. (play, scribble)

8. Then she _____ her scribbles many different colors. (color, carry)

9. Her mother _____ to guess what the drawings were. (try, pick)

10. After she grew up, Pat _____ about art jobs. (like, learn)

Extension: Have students write five sentences using the past tense of the verbs they didn't choose in the above sentences.

Future Tense

- A verb in the future tense tells about an action that is going to happen.

- To write about the future, use the special verb *will*.

Underline the action verb in each sentence. Rewrite the sentence so it tells about the future.

1. Two friends go to art school.

_____

2. They draw every day.

_____

3. The art students use watercolors.

_____

4. The students paint pictures with oil paint.

_____

5. Some artists illustrate books.

_____

6. Other artists create drawings on computers.

_____

7. Many artists teach art.

_____

8. Most artists notice things around them.

_____

Extension: Encourage students to think of a job they might do in the future. Ask students to write four sentences telling what they will do as part of their job.

Grade 4/Unit 3
Pat Cummings: My Story

8

McGraw-Hill School Division

Past and Future Tenses

- A verb in the past tense tells about an action that already happened.

- Add -ed to most verbs to show past tense.

- A verb in the future tense tells about an action that is going to happen.

- To write about the future, use the special verb *will*.

Read each sentence. Underline the verb that is in the incorrect tense.
Write the correct tense.

1. In a few days, Pat Cummings visit our library. _____

2. Yesterday Carla will walk to the library. _____

3. She borrow a book yesterday with illustrations by Pat Cummings.

   _____

4. Carla returned the book tomorrow. _____

5. Last year, Carla will mail a letter to Pat Cummings. _____

6. Tomorrow she send a picture to Pat Cummings. _____

7. Carla already paint the picture. _____

8. Next month, another artist come to the library. _____

8 Grade 4 / Unit 3
Pat Cummings: My Story

Extension: Invite groups of students to look for past-tense verbs in newspapers or magazines. Ask students to copy the sentences they find and then rewrite the sentences, using future-tense verbs.

73

Letter Punctuation and Capitalization

> - Begin the greeting and closing in a letter with a capital letter.
>
> - Use a comma after the greeting and the closing in a letter.
>
> - Use a comma between the names of a city and a state.
>
> - Use a comma between the day and year in a date.

Read the letter carefully. Correct two capitalization mistakes. Also add six missing commas.

June 22 2000

108 Oak Avenue
Audubon IA 50025

Janell Washington
16 Longwood Drive
Chicago IL 60640

dear Janell

In school, I read a story about an artist Named Pat Cummings. I enjoyed it very much. When she was young, she loved to draw pictures. Sometimes she traded pictures with kids in her class.

I will go to camp next week in Bear Creek Michigan. I will send you a postcard from there. Then I will give you my camp address. I hope you will write to me.

your friend
Sam

McGraw-Hill School Division

Past and Future Tenses

A. Rewrite each underlined verb, using the correct past-tense form.

1. When Pat Cummings was five years old, she disappear for an afternoon.

   _____

2. Her mother call the army police. _____

3. The dance teacher pin a note on Pat. _____

4. As a child, Pat Cummings like to draw ballerinas. _____

5. When she grew up, Pat Cummings study art. _____

B. Choose a verb from the box below to complete each sentence. Write the future-tense form of the verb.

fetch	get	look	remember	work

6. Sometimes Pat Cummings _____ ideas when she is

   swimming.

7. Pat Cummings _____ at night if she has an idea.

8. When she travels, she _____ at people around her.

9. Pat's cat _____ when Pat throws a toy.

10. Pat always _____ how Tom Feelings helped her.

Past and Future Tenses

- Add *-ed* to most verbs to show past tense.
- If a verb ends with *e*, drop the *e* and add *-ed*.
- If a verb ends with a consonant and *y*, change *y* to *i* and add *-ed*.
- If a verb ends with one vowel and one consonant, double the consonant and add *-ed*.
- To write about the future, use the special verb *will*.

Mechanics:

- Begin the greeting and closing in a letter with a capital letter.
- Use a comma after the greeting and the closing in a letter.
- Use a comma between the name of a city and a state.
- Use a comma between the day and year in a date.

Change each underlined verb to the correct past or future tense. Also add any missing commas and correct the capitalization mistakes.

February 5 2000

333 Coronado Court
Modesto CA 95350

Alberto Rivera
789 Prairie Street
Fort Wayne IN 46815

hi Alberto

Yesterday, I <u>try</u> _____ to draw a picture of my dog. At first, he

<u>move</u> _____ so much, I couldn't do it. Then I <u>pet</u>

_____ him a lot, and he sat still. When I grow up, I <u>paint</u>

_____ beautiful paintings. Someday, I <u>draw</u>

_____ pictures for children's books, too.

your cousin
Marco

Main and Helping Verbs

> • The **main verb** in a sentence shows what the subject does or is.
>
> • A **helping verb** helps the main verb show an action or make a statement.
>
> • *Have, has,* and *had* are helping verbs.

Draw one line under each form of *has* that is a helping verb. Draw two lines under each main verb that it helps.

1. Basho got his name after he had planted a banana tree.

2. Basho has decided upon a trip across Japan.

3. When he had prepared for his trip, Basho left home.

4. Before leaving, Basho had stitched a string on his hat to keep it from blowing away.

5. The cherry blossoms have waited for Basho.

6. The poet has scribbled some words on his hat.

7. An old woman has invited Basho to share her noodles.

8. Basho's friends have joined him for part of the trip.

9. They have presented Basho with presents for his trip.

10. Basho left his friends after they had crossed the river.

Grade 4/Unit 3
Grass Sandals: The Travels of Basho

Extension: Ask students to write *has, have,* and *had* on separate index cards. Have them work in small groups, each choosing a card and constructing an oral sentence that uses the form chosen as a helping verb.

More Main and Helping Verbs

- *Is, are, am, was*, and *were* can be helping verbs.

- They are used with a main verb ending in *-ing*

- *Will* is a helping verb used to help show an action in the future.

Read each sentence. Study the helping verb. Circle the correct form of the main verb in parentheses.

1. Basho's friends were (wave, waving) as they left in the boat.

2. As he stands under a waterfall, Basho is (laugh, laughing).

3. Soon Basho's feet will (take, taking) him past an old temple.

4. The beautiful cherry trees are (bloom, blooming).

5. During his trip, Basho was (sleep, sleeping) in huts, houses, and stalls.

6. Most of the time, the poet —————— walking. (is, are).

7. Tomorrow Basho will (ride, riding) on a farmer's horse.

8. Along the way, people are (give, giving) Basho food.

Extension: Ask students to write three sentences that begin with "I am" and tell what they are doing right now.

Grade 4/Unit 3
Grass Sandals: The Travels of Basho

/8

Using Main and Helping Verbs to Complete Sentences

- The **main verb** in a sentence shows what the subject does or is.

- A **helping verb** helps the main verb show an action or make a statement.

- *Have, has,* and *had* can be helping verbs.

- *Is, are, am, was, were* and *will* can be helping verbs.

Write a main verb or helping verb to complete each sentence.

1. Basho has ——————— rice and beans into balls.

2. Basho had ——————— rice and beans last night.

3. Now Basho ——————— meeting with some friends.

4. As they drink tea, the friends ——————— looking in their cups.

5. Last night, they were ——————— poems together.

6. Tomorrow, Basho ——————— leave his friends.

7. They ——————— enjoyed their time together.

8. Basho saw many of the animals that ——————— living in the fields.

9. One night, Basho heard a frog that ——————— jumping into a pond.

10. By the end of his trip, Basho had ——————— to many places.

10   Grade 4/Unit 3
Grass Sandals: The Travels of Basho

Extension: Have students read a few paragraphs in a favorite book. Ask them to write down five combinations of main and helping verbs they find in the book.

79

Contractions

- A **contraction** is a shortened form of two words.

- A contraction can be made by combining a verb with the word *not*.

- An apostrophe (') shows the letter *o* has been left out.

Read each sentence. Write the contraction for each set of underlined words.

1. Haiku poems <u>are not</u> rhyming poems. —————

2. Perhaps you <u>have not</u> seen poems like them before. —————

3. Basho <u>is not</u> the name that the poet was given at birth. —————

4. Basho <u>did not</u> travel by car. —————

5. Basho <u>was not</u> a Chinese poet. —————

6. His friends <u>would not</u> let him leave empty-handed. —————

7. The poet <u>did not</u> forget his morning tea. —————

8. Basho <u>had not</u> walked far when he saw a waterfall. —————

9. Basho's shoelaces <u>were not</u> white. —————

10. Even though Basho lived long ago, his poems <u>have not</u> been forgotten.

—————

Extension: Arrange students in pairs. Give each student twelve index cards. Have one partner write the underlined words from this page on cards. Have the other write the contractions on cards. Invite partners to play a game in which they match the contractions with the longer forms.

80

Grade 4/Unit 3
Grass Sandals: The Travels of Basho 10

Main and Helping Verbs

A. Read each sentence. Draw one line under the helping verb and two lines under the main verb.

1. After he had laced on a new pair of sandals, Basho took another walk.

2. Basho wrote a poem about flowers that were blooming.

3. Today people are visiting the places that Basho knew.

4. Long after Basho lived, people are reading his poems.

5. Throughout history, poets like Basho have helped us to appreciate nature.

B. Choose the correct helping verb to complete each sentence. Write it on the line.

6. I ——————— writing a haiku poem.

   a. am

   b. are

   c. will

7. Our teacher ——————— put our poems on a bulletin board tomorrow.

   a. have

   b. was

   c. will

8. We ——————— painted pictures to go with our poems.

   a. are

   b. have

   c. were

Main and Helping Verbs

- The **main verb** in a sentence shows what the subject does or is.
- A **helping verb** helps the main verb show an action or make a statement.
- *Have, has,* and *had* can be helping verbs.
- *Is, are, am, was, were,* and *will* can be helping verbs.

Mechanics:

- A contraction is a shortened form of two words.
- A contraction can be made by combining a verb with the word *not*.
- An apostrophe (') shows the letter *o* has been left out.

Look at the picture. Proofread the paragraph. Correct mistakes in main verbs and helping verbs. Change the underlined words to contractions. Rewrite the paragraph on the lines.

    In many poems, Basho was write about animals. In one of his poems, a crab are tickling his leg. In another poem, a horse have chewed a flower. <u>Was not</u> there a poem in this story about a frog? Basho <u>is not</u> alive today, but you can read his poems.

_____

_____

_____

_____

_____

Linking Verts

> • A **linking verb** does not show action. It connects the subject to the rest of the sentence.
>
> • *Is, are, am, was,* and *were* are often used as linking verbs.

Read each sentence. Study the linking verbs in parentheses. Write the form of the linking verb that correctly completes each sentence.

1. The Big Dipper ——————— a group of stars. (is, are)

2. The children's names ——————— James and Lettie. (was, were)

3. Papa's new name ——————— Starman. (was, were)

4. Indiana ——————— the state where the family made their home. (is, are)

5. Barns and beds ——————— things that Papa can build. (is, are)

6. James thought Mama's cooking ——————— just wonderful. (was, were)

7. Mama and the children ——————— worried when Papa was away.

   (was, were)

8. The children certainly ——————— happy when Papa returns. (is, are)

9. Papa's relatives ——————— eager to leave the plantation. (was, were)

10. You ——————— older than James and Lettie. (am, are)

Extension: Ask students to write a paragraph describing the town of Freedom. Urge them to use linking verbs in their description. Invite students to share their descriptions.

Linking Verbs

> • Some linking verbs link the subject to a noun in the predicate.
>
> • Some linking verbs link the subject to an adjective in the predicate.

Read each sentence. Circle the linking verb that links the subject to a noun or adjective in the predicate. Underline the noun or adjective.

1. Lettie was wriggly as a child.

2. Lettie's older brother, James, was tall.

3. Some people leaving Tennessee were runaways from plantations.

4. The travelers were weary from their long walk.

5. The face of the old fisherman is wrinkled.

6. How many of the new settlers are farmers?

7. Mama was the teacher in the village school.

8. A few people in the village were carpenters.

9. The vegetables that the boy raises are beans.

10. The name of the village is Freedom.

84

Extension: Have students identify whether each linking verb that they underlined in these sentences is in the present tense or the past tense.

Grade 4/Unit 3
A Place Called Freedom (10)

Writing Linking Verbs to Complete Sentences

- A linking verb does not show action. It connects the subject to the rest of the sentence.
- *Is, are, am, was,* and *were* are often used as linking verbs.
- Some linking verbs link the subject to a noun in the predicate.
- Some linking verbs link the subject to an adjective in the predicate.

Complete each sentence by writing the correct linking verb on the line. Then underline the complete subject of the sentence.

1. Scott Russell Sanders —————— an author.

2. Writing, nature, and towns —————— the author's favorite things.

3. Mr. Sanders —————— a college teacher these days as well as an author.

4. His birthplace —————— a big city in Tennessee.

5. His favorite subjects for writing —————— people who get along.

6. Thomas B. Allen —————— nine years old when he went to an art class.

7. Streetcars —————— his way of getting to class back then.

8. The other people in the class —————— adults.

9. As an adult, Allen —————— eager to look for ideas in libraries.

10. The countryside —————— another good place for finding ideas.

Extension: Arrange students in small groups. Have students write *is, are, am, was,* and *were* on index cards and turn the cards facedown. Then invite students to take turns picking a card and using the linking verb in an oral sentence.

Titles

- Capitalize the first and last words and all important words in the titles of books and newspapers.

- Underline titles of books, newspapers, magazines, and TV series.

- Put quotation marks around the titles of short stories, articles, songs, poems, and book chapters.

Rewrite each sentence making sure the titles are written correctly.

1. A newspaper in Freedom might be called the freedom times.

_____

2. James could have written a book called my life in freedom, indiana.

_____

3. The song amazing grace is about slavery.

_____

4. Have you seen the TV series the end of slavery?

_____

5. Did you read the magazine article the freedom train?

_____

6. walking to freedom is a poem that my friend Dara wrote.

_____

Extension: Have students work in pairs. One student writes four titles without capital letters, underlining, or quotation marks. The other student writes the titles correctly. Then students reverse roles and repeat the activity.

Grade 4/Unit 3
A Place Called Freedom 6

Linking Verbs

A. Find the linking verb in each sentence. Write it on the line.

1. The year 1832 was the year the family left the plantation.

_____

2., Papa, Mama, and James were the family members who walked.

_____

3. I am amazed that they traveled so far on foot.

_____

4. When the family reaches Indiana, the hills are white with flowers.

_____

B. Find the noun or adjective in the predicate that is linked to the subject by a linking verb. Write it on the line.

5. A Quaker family was kind to the travelers from Tennessee.

_____

6. The Starman family is glad to help with their farm work.

_____

7. Papa was a farmer and planted corn and wheat the first year.

_____

8. Potatoes and beans were the vegetables that James planted.

_____

Linking Verbs

- A **linking verb** does not show action. It connects the subject to the rest of the sentence.

- *Is, are, am, was*, and *were* are often used as linking verbs.

- Some linking verbs link the subject to a noun in the predicate.

- Some linking verbs link the subject to an adjective in the predicate.

Mechanics:

- Capitalize the first and last words and all important words in the titles of books and newspapers.

- Underline titles of books, newspapers, magazines, and TV series.

- Put quotation marks around the titles of short stories, articles, songs, poems, and book chapters.

Work with a partner. Take turns reading the following paragraph aloud. Listen for mistakes in linking verbs. Think about which words are titles. Decide together what corrections need to be made and rewrite the paragraph correctly.

     Our social studies book is social studies today. The books is new. The title of yesterday's chapter were slavery in the south. I are ready to give a report today. I wrote a poem about slavery that I call freedom.

_____

_____

_____

_____

Irregular Verbs

•	An **irregular verb** is a verb that does not add *-ed* to form the past tense.

Write the correct past-tense form of the underlined verb on the line provided.

1. Adrian Fisher <u>begin</u> _____ to make mazes more than 20 years ago.

2. Fisher <u>make</u> _____ a huge maze in 1996.

3. This maze <u>break</u> _____ the record for the largest maze.

4. About 2,000 people <u>find</u> _____ their way through it in one day.

5. Adults as well as children <u>come</u> _____ to try the maze.

6. Children <u>go</u> _____ through the maze faster than their parents.

7. Fisher <u>do</u> _____ a special maze to honor a Beatles song.

8. A plane <u>fly</u> _____ over Adrian Fisher's mazes.

9. An artist <u>draw</u> _____ pictures of the mazes.

10. The drawings show what the pilot <u>see</u> _____.

Extension: Have students work with partners to find examples of irregular past-tense verbs in newspaper articles. Ask students to make and share a list of the verbs they find.

Irregular Verbs

- Some irregular verbs have special spellings when used with the helping verb *have, has,* or *had*.

Read each sentence and the verb choices in parentheses. Underline the verb choice that correctly completes the sentence.

1. Adrian Fisher has (built, builded) more than 135 mazes.

2. He has (did, done) mazes in England and the United States.

3. Fisher had (make, made) the maze in Michigan in the shape of a car.

4. The cornstalks in his corn maze have (grew, grown) high.

5. He had (lay, laid) out the Beatles maze in the shape of a submarine.

6. This maze master has (put, putted) roadblocks in his mazes.

7. Sometimes there have (were, been) live crocodiles in his mazes, too.

8. Thousands of people have (seen, saw) Fisher's mazes.

9. He has (taken, took) a lot of care with his designs.

10. People have (begun, began) to take maze design seriously.

Irregular Verbs

- An **irregular verb** is a verb that does not add -ed to form the past tense.
- Some irregular verbs have special spellings when used with the helping verb *have, has,* or *had*.

Rewrite each sentence with the correct form of the underlined verb. For each sentence, use the form that makes better sense—the past-tense form or the past with the helping verb *have, has,* or *had*.

1. One time I <u>go</u> through a maze.

_____

2. I wonder if you have ever <u>go</u> through a maze.

_____

3. I <u>know</u> there was a rule for going through a maze.

_____

4. I followed the rule and <u>find</u> that it worked!

_____

5. The left wall had <u>lead</u> me back to the path.

_____

6. Finally I <u>see</u> the way out of the maze.

_____

7. The maze had <u>keep</u> me busy for quite a while.

_____

8. Did you know that Adrian Fisher has <u>break</u> the rule of maze making?

_____

Grade 4/Unit 3
Twisted Trails

Extension: Arrange students in groups. Ask each group to make a chart with three columns labeled *Present Tense, Past Tense,* and *Past with Have, Has, or Had.* Have students fill in the columns with forms for the verbs in parentheses.

Abbreviations

- An abbreviation is the shortened form of a word.

- An abbreviation begins with a capital letter and ends with a period.

- Abbreviate titles of people before names. You can abbreviate days of the week.

- You can also abbreviate most months.

Rewrite this invitation by writing each underlined abbreviation correctly.

Dear Jesse,

Would you like to go through <u>mr</u> Fisher's maze with us? My mother says that we will go on <u>sat</u>, <u>nov</u> 10. Derek and <u>mrs</u> Long are coming. I went to see <u>dr</u> Ortega on <u>thurs</u>, and he showed me how to brush my teeth better. I'll call you tomorrow afternoon.

Sam

_____

_____

_____

_____

_____

Extension: Have pairs of students quiz each other on abbreviations. Have one partner write a word and the other write the abbreviation.

92

Grade 4/Unit 3
Twisted Trails 6

Irregular Verbs

A. Circle the letter before the irregular verb that correctly completes each sentence.

1. Our class ___ reading about mazes yesterday.

    a. begin

    b. began

    c. begun

    d. beginned

2. We ___ some mazes on paper.

    a. draw

    b. drawed

    c. drew

    d. drawn

B. Circle the letter before the correct irregular verb and helping verb that completes each sentence.

3. The maze master ___ a maze with three miles of paths in it.

    a. has made

    b. has make

    c. had make

    d. have made

4. Adults ___ lost in Adrian Fisher's mazes.

    a. has became

    b. has become

    c. have became

    d. have become

Irregular Verbs

> • An **irregular verb** is a verb that does not add *-ed* to form the past tense.
>
> • Some irregular verbs have special spellings when used with the helping verb *have, has,* or *had.*

Mechanics

> • An abbreviation is the shortened form of a word. An abbreviation begins with a capital letter and ends with a period.
>
> • Abbreviate titles of people before names. You can abbreviate days of the week and most months.

Read the sentences about the picture below. Change the verbs that are not written correctly. Put capital letters and periods where they belong in the abbreviations. Rewrite the sentences on the lines below.

1. The students in ms Ming's class have drew a circular maze.

   _____

2. Last week they taked their maze to mr Johnson's class.

   _____

3. This morning mrs Green's class come to see the maze.

   _____

4. Later they gave the maze to the principal, dr Miller.

   _____

5. Now everyone in the school has see the maze.

   _____

Verbs

Read each passage and look at the underlined parts. Is there a better way to write and say each part? If there is, which is the better way? Circle your answer.

The hatmaker sit write, and draws. He creates a sign for his shop. He
      (1)

shows the sign to several people. They tells him to make changes.
                       (2)

The hatmaker rushes back to his shop and makes a new sign.

---

1. **A** The hatmaker sat, writes, and draws.

   B The hatmaker sits, wrote, and draws.

   C The hatmaker sits, writes, and draws.

   D No mistake

2. **F** Them told him to make changes.

   G They told he to make changes.

   H They tell him to make changes.

   J No mistake

December 1, 2000
777 Forest Street
Orange, MA 01364

Chris Little
129 Blueberry Circle
York, ME 03909

Dear Chris,
I looked at some books with drawings by Pat Cummings. She liked to draw when she was young. Then she study art and became an artist. I think I
                                             (3)
will study art, too.

your's friend,
  (4)
Lucas

---

3. **A** Then her study art and became an artist.

   B Then she studyed art and become an artist.

   C Then she studied art and became an artist.

   D No mistake

4. **F** Your friend,

   G You're friend,

   H Your's friend,

   J No mistake

Verbs

Basho is preparing to walk across Japan. <u>He isnt taken much with him.</u>
(5)
Basho is a poet, and he will write poems during his journey. <u>His friends</u>
<u>has given him a pair of sandals paper, and ink.</u>
(6)

---

5. **A** He isnt taking much with him.
   B He isn't taken much with he.
   C He isn't taking much with him.
   D No mistake

6. **F** His friend's have gave him a pair of sandals, paper, and ink.
   G His friends have given him a pair of sandals, paper, and ink.
   H His friend have given him a pair of sandals, paper, and ink.
   J No mistake

Each group in my class wrote a song about the town of Freedom. <u>My group's</u>
(7)
<u>song is called "A Place to Be Free."</u> All the groups sang their songs to the
class. <u>Ms. Brady said our songs was wonderful.</u>
(8)

---

7. **A** my group's song is called "a place to be free."
   B My group song is called A Place to Be Free.
   C My groups song is called "A Place to Be Free."
   D No mistake

8. **F** Ms Brady said our song's is wonderful.
   G Ms. brady says our songs was wonderful.
   H Ms. Brady said our songs were wonderful.
   J No mistake

<u>Dee write a list of things to do for the week.</u> <u>heres her list:</u> 1. Mon.—Read
(9)   (10)
article about mazes. 2. Tues.—Visit magazine's Web site. 3. Wed.—Get book
of mazes from library. 4. Thurs.—Draw my own maze. 5. Fri.—Show my maze
to Cathy.

---

9. **A** Dee has wrote a list of things to do for the week.
   B dee has written a list of things to do for the week
   C Dee has written a list of things to do for the week.
   D No mistake

10. **F** Here's her list:
    G Hear's her list:
    H Heres her list:
    J No mistake

Adjectives

> • An **adjective** is a word that describes a noun.
>
> • An adjective tells what kind or how many.

Choose an adjective from the box below that correctly fits in the sentence.
Then write your answer on the line provided.

all	cold	most	several	silly	six	strong	superior	two	white

1. Scruffy lives in a very ——————— place.

2. A wolf pack is a family of ——————— wolves of different ages.

3. There are ——————— leaders of Scruffy's wolf pack.

4. ——————— alpha wolves get to eat first after a hunt.

5. ——————— male wolves leave their parents when they grow up.

6. A ——————— Scruffy has trouble getting food to eat.

7. In the summer, ——————— wolf pups are born.

8. With Scruffy's help, the pups become ——————— wolves.

9. To the pups, Scruffy is a ——————— wolf.

10. Wolves with ——————— fur are hard to see in the snow.

10 Grade 4 / Unit 4
Scruffy

Extension: Ask students to choose their favorite wild
animal and write a description of it. Have students
use adjectives that tell what kind or how many.

97

Adjectives and Linking Verbs

- An adjective can come after the noun it describes.

- The noun and adjective are connected by a linking verb.

Read each sentence. Underline each linking verb, and then write the adjective that comes after the noun on the line provided.

1. Scruffy is timid. —————

2. The other wolves were bold and good hunters. —————

3. Alpha wolves are strong and attack first. —————

4. Soon the pups were big and running around. —————

5. Scruffy was perky when he was with the pups. —————

6. Arctic wolves are gray during the summer. —————

7. Their fur is white during the winter. —————

8. The pups' mother was gentle. —————

9. This female wolf is good-natured. —————

10. The baby pups were tiny. —————

Extension: Have students write four sentences about members of their family, using linking verbs and adjectives after the nouns.

98

Grade 4/ Unit 4
Scruffy
10

Adjectives

> • An adjective tells *what kind* or *how many*.
>
> • An adjective can come after the noun it describes.

Underline the adjective in each sentence. Decide if the adjective tells *what kind* or *how many*, and then write *what kind* or *how many* on the line provided.

1. The weather on Ellesmere Island is snowy. _____

2. Huge icebergs surround the island. _____

3. Some wolves in a wolf pack are brothers and sisters. _____

4. Sometimes Scruffy was a confused wolf. _____

5. Most wolves in the pack hunted. _____

6. One wolf usually did not go on the hunt. _____

7. Watchful Scruffy was the pups' baby-sitter. _____

8. With Scruffy, the pups were playful. _____

9. There were four pups in the litter. _____

10. The opening into the den was narrow. _____

McGraw-Hill School Division

10

Grade 4 / Unit 4
Scruffy

Extension: Ask students to listen as you read a few paragraphs about the Arctic. Have students write down five or more adjectives that they hear.

Proper Adjectives

> • **Proper adjectives** are formed from proper nouns.
>
> • A proper adjective begins with a capital letter.

Rewrite each sentence. Write each proper adjective correctly.

1. Jim Brandenburg filmed wolves for a national geographic television show.

_____

2. To some native american people, the wolf is a special animal.

_____

3. Brandenburg has taken many photographs of arctic animals.

_____

4. The atlantic walrus lives in the Arctic.

_____

5. The iceland tern is another animal that lives in this region.

_____

6. Various eskimo tribes have lived in this part of the world.

_____

7. Jim Brandenburg and his family live in the minnesota woods.

_____

8. Part of this state is on the canadian border.

_____

Extension: Have students work in pairs to look through
science or social studies books and list any proper
adjectives they find.

Grade 4/Unit 4
Scruffy

8

Adjectives

A. Write *yes* if the underlined word in the sentence is an adjective. Write *no* if it is not an adjective.

1. Arctic wolves live where there are fields of <u>snow</u>.

   _____

2. The wolf was named Scruffy because he was <u>messy</u>.

   _____

3. Scruffy and the pups played with a piece of <u>fur</u>.

   _____

4. Scruffy wanted the eggs of some <u>Arctic</u> birds.

   _____

B. Find the adjective in each sentence. Then write your answer on the line.

5. Sometimes Scruffy was mean and bullied the pups.

   _____

6. Scruffy often took the frisky pups on walks.

   _____

7. The six pups happily followed Scruffy.

   _____

8. The climate of Ellesmere Island is harsh.

   _____

Adjectives

- An **adjective** is a word that describes a noun.

- An adjective tells *what kind* or *how many*.

- An adjective can come after the noun it describes.

- The noun and adjective are connected by a linking verb.

- Proper adjectives are formed from proper nouns.

- A proper adjective begins with a capital letter.

Use the adjectives in the box to complete the sentences.

Arctic	**gray**	**long**	**sharp**	**six**	**tall**	**two**

1. The _____ region has _____ icebergs.

2. The color of the _____ pups Scruffy cared for was _____.

3. _____ pups like to hold a _____ stick in their mouths.

4. Scruffy growls at the pups and shows his _____ teeth.

Articles

> • The words *a, an*, and *the* are special adjectives called **articles**.
>
> • Use *a* and *an* with singular nouns.
>
> • Use *a* if the next word starts with a consonant sound.
>
> • Use *an* if the next word starts with a vowel sound.

Complete each sentence by writing the correct article, **a** or **an**.

1. Gluskabe was ——————— good giant.

2. Long ago, Skunk was ——————— animal with white fur.

3. Gluskabe and Skunk went on ——————— difficult journey.

4. Some people were in trouble because of ——————— deep snowfall.

5. Skunk became ——————— angry creature during the trip.

6. Gluskabe spoke to ——————— large bird with white feathers.

7. On the way home, Skunk saw ——————— eagle.

8. Skunk tied Day Eagle's wings with ——————— piece of twine.

9. Today the skunk has ——————— black coat with white stripes.

10. He also has ——————— odor that nobody likes.

11. He is ——————— animal that people try to avoid.

12. If you see ——————— skunk, don't scare him!

12
Grade 4 / Unit 4
Gluskabe and the Snow Bird

Extension: Have students write and share at least one riddle about animals, using *a* and *an* in their clues.

103

More Articles

- Use *the* with singular nouns that name a particular person, place, or thing.

- Use *the* before all plural nouns.

Read each sentence. Then underline each article once and underline the noun that each article points out twice.

1. Skunk and Gluskabe walked north to see the Snow Bird.

2. They went to solve the problem of too much snow.

3. The snowbird lived on a hilltop.

4. When snow melts, it fills the rivers.

5. Snow protects the plants in winter.

6. Too much snow was causing an impossible problem for hunters.

7. Skunk wanted to be an important person.

8. Skunk tied the Day Eagle's wings.

9. Gluskabe gave Skunk a harsh punishment.

10. Gluskabe drew the white stripes that skunks have today.

Extension: Have each student write a paragraph telling what they know or have heard about skunks. Then have students exchange papers and circle the articles *a, an,* and *the* in the paragraphs they receive.

Grade 4/Unit 4
Gluskabe and the Snow Bird
10

Articles

> • Use *a* and *an* with singular nouns.
> • Use *a* if the next word starts with a consonant sound.
> • Use *an* if the next word starts with a vowel sound.
> • Use *the* with singular nouns that name a particular person, place, or thing.
> • Use *the* before all plural nouns.

Each sentence is missing two articles. Add the articles and then write the sentences correctly.

1. Skunk was excellent cook so he prepared meals.

   _____

2. In the old days, all of animals admired Skunk because he had beautiful coat.

   _____

3. One day messenger came to see Great One.

   _____

4. Gluskabe made enormous footprint in snow.

   _____

5. Skunk thought giant Snow Bird was amazing creature.

   _____

6. Another bird was standing at top of hill.

   _____

7. Skunk did evil thing to bird called Day Eagle.

   _____

8. During night, Skunk tied wings of this great bird.

   _____

8 Grade 4/Unit 4
Gluskabe and the Snow Bird

Extension: Ask students to write a few sentences explaining what Gluskabe did to punish Skunk. Remind students to use articles correctly.

105

Quotations

> • Use quotation marks at the beginning and end of a person's exact words.
>
> • Begin a quotation with a capital letter.
>
> • Do not use quotation marks when you do not use the speaker's exact words.

Rewrite each sentence correctly by putting capital letters and quotation marks where they belong.

1. Mr. Peterson asked, did you like the story about Gluskabe?

_____

2. we liked it very much, the students answered.

_____

3. then let's put on a play about it, the teacher said.

_____

4. Mr. Peterson looked around and said, James, you can play Skunk.

_____

5. that's great! James replied with a grin.

_____

6. Grace raised her hand and asked, could I be the Snow Bird?

_____

7. Mr. Peterson said, sure, if it's O.K. with the rest of the class.

_____

8. The other students said that it was a great idea.

_____

Extension: Have students write three more sentences about Mr. Peterson and the play. Tell students to put quotations in each sentence. Students can exchange sentences and proofread a partner's work for correct quotation style.

Grade 4/Unit 4
Gluskabe and the Snow Bird

8

Articles

A. Circle the letter before the sentence that uses articles correctly.

1. **a.** Gluskabe was an giant.
    b. Gluskabe was a good giant.
    c. Gluskabe untied a knots.

2. **a.** Skunk was the giant's cook.
    b. Skunk once was an white animal.
    c. Skunk sank in a footprints.

3. **a.** Skunk saw an big bird.
    b. The Day Eagle closed his wings.
    c. People could not see in a dark.

4. **a.** Gluskabe used an ashes from the fire.
    b. Skunk sleeps in a winter.
    c. People did not like the smell.

B. Circle the letter before the article that correctly completes each sentence.

5. Skunk watched snowflakes fall from ___ bird's wings.
    a. a
    b. an
    c. the

6. Skunk wanted to do ___ awesome thing.
    a. a
    b. an
    c. the

7. Skunk cooked ___ delicious meal for Gluskabe.
    a. a
    b. an
    c. the

8. Now skunks have ___very bad smell.
    a. the
    b. an
    c. a

Articles and Quotations

- The words *a, an,* and *the* are special adjectives called **articles**.

- Use *a* and *an* with singular nouns. Use *a* if the next word starts with a consonant sound. Use *an* if the next word starts with a vowel sound.

- Use *the* with singular nouns that name a particular person, place, or thing.

- Use *the* before all plural nouns.

Mechanics

- Use quotation marks at the beginning and end of a person's exact words.

- Begin a quotation with a capital letter.

Read each sentence aloud and decide which underlined word is correct.
Then rewrite the sentence, putting quotation marks and capital letters where they belong.

1. Roy asked, do you know what color Skunk was in <u>the</u>, <u>an</u> old days?

_____

2. Tia said, he had <u>a</u>, <u>an</u> pretty white coat.

_____

3. later Gluskabe turned <u>the</u>, <u>a</u> skunk's coat black, Tia explained.

_____

4. then Gluskabe gave him <u>a</u>, <u>an</u> ugly smell, Roy said.

_____

Adjectives That Compare

- Add -*er* to most adjectives to compare two people, places, or things.

- Add -*est* to most adjectives to compare more than two.

Read each sentence. Underline the adjective in parentheses that correctly completes the sentence.

1. Sylvia Earle hopes to dive to the (deeper, deepest) part of the ocean.

2. The water at the surface is (brighter, brightest) than the water down below.

3. The bottom is the (darker, darkest) part of the ocean.

4. The water past the waves is (deeper, deepest) than the water by the shore.

5. The Florida waters were (cleaner, cleanest) in the past than they are today.

6. Sharks are (faster, fastest) swimmers than people.

7. The Jim Suit is a (newer, newest) invention than scuba gear.

8. People wearing Jim Suits are (slower, slowest) swimmers than dolphins.

9. Of all work, Sylvia believes exploring the ocean is the (greater, greatest).

10. She thinks sea creatures are some of the (grander, grandest) animals in the world.

Extension: Write each adjective in parentheses on an index card. Have students take turns drawing a card from a hat or bowl, and then use the adjective in a sentence of their own.

Adjectives That Compare

- For adjectives ending in *e*, drop the *e* before adding *-er* or *-est*.

- For adjectives ending in a consonant and *y*, change the *y* to *i* before adding *-er* or *-est*.

- For adjectives that have a single vowel before a final consonant, double the final consonant before adding *-er* or *-est*.

Complete each sentence by writing the correct form of the adjective in parentheses.

1. As a child, Sylvia's (happy) _____ times were spent under water.

2. Of the many sea creatures, some of the (strange) _____ ones live on the bottom of the ocean.

3. The poisonous lionfish is one of the (deadly) _____ animals in the sea.

4. Dolphins are (friendly) _____ than sharks.

5. Humpback whales are (big) _____ than sharks.

6. The blue whale is the (large) _____ living animal.

7. A scorpionfish is (scary) _____ than a dolphin.

8. Scuba gear is (clumsy) _____ than a one-person sub.

9. Even the (tiny) _____ plants in the ocean make oxygen.

10. Pollution is one of the (sad) _____ things people have done to the sea.

110

Extension: Have students choose three sea creatures to compare in sentences, using adjectives to make the comparisons. Tell students to write four sentences.

Grade 4/Unit 4
Meet an Underwater Explorer
10

Adjectives That Compare

- Add *-er* to most adjectives to compare two people, places, or things.
- Add *-est* to most adjectives to compare more than two.
- For adjectives ending in *e*, drop the *e* before adding *-er* or *-est*.
- For adjectives ending in a consonant and *y*, change the *y* to *i* before adding *-er* or *-est*.
- For adjectives that have a single vowel before a final consonant, double the final consonant before adding *-er* or *-est*.

Rewrite the sentences below, correcting the form or spelling of the underlined adjective.

1. There is no light in the <u>deeppest</u> part of the sea.

_____

2. At the bottom of the sea, food is <u>scarcest</u> than at the top.

_____

3. The great white shark is <u>smallier</u> than a whale shark.

_____

4. The whale shark is the <u>bigger</u> of all sharks.

_____

5. The teeth of some sharks are <u>sharpest</u> than razor blades.

_____

6. One of the <u>flatter</u> animals in the sea is the ray.

_____

6 Grade 4/Unit 4
Meet an Underwater Explorer

Extension: Ask students to make a chart of five different adjectives to compare by adding *-er* and *-est*. Have students write the three forms of each adjective, such as *hot, hotter, hottest*.

111

Proper Adjectives

> • Proper adjectives are formed from proper nouns.
>
> • A proper adjective or proper noun begins with a capital letter.

Rewrite each sentence using each proper adjective and proper noun correctly.

1. The diving suit sylvia earle wore was named for a british diver.

_____

2. His name was jim jarrett, and the suit was called a jim suit.

_____

3. It was in hawaiian waters that Sylvia walked on the bottom of the pacific ocean.

_____

4. Sylvia is an american diver who lived in florida as a child.

_____

5. Sylvia has worked for the united states government as a scientist.

_____

Extension: Have students, working in groups, list proper adjectives and proper nouns that they find in newspapers and magazines. Encourage groups to find as many as they can within a set period of time.

Grade 4/Unit 4
Meet an Underwater Explorer 5

Adjectives That Compare

A. Read each sentence. Write *yes* if the underlined adjective is the correct form or correct spelling. Write *no* if it is not the correct form or correct spelling.

1. Of all the fish, Luis thought the lantern fish was the <u>funnyest</u>.

   _____

2. Sara Ann thinks the sea horse is the <u>cutest</u> sea animal.

   _____

3. Some starfish have <u>shorter</u> arms than others.

   _____

4. A jellyfish has a <u>thiner</u> body than an octopus.

   _____

B. Read each sentence. Use the correct form of the adjective in parentheses. Write it on the line.

5. Scuba gear is (heavy) —————— than snorkeling equipment.

6. Sylvia's practice dive was in (shallow) —————— water than her real dive.

7. Underwater divers get to see the (rare) —————— creatures of the sea.

8. The red starfish is the (red) —————— of all starfish.

Adjectives That Compare

- Add *-er* to most adjectives to compare two people, places, or things.

- Add *-est* to most adjectives to compare more than two.

- For adjectives ending in *e*, drop the *e* before adding *-er* or *-est*.

- For adjectives ending in a consonant and *y*, change the *y* to *i* before adding *-er* or *-est*.

- For adjectives that have a single vowel before a final consonant, double the final consonant before adding *-er* or *-est*.

Mechanics

- Proper adjectives are formed from proper nouns.

- A proper adjective or proper noun begins with a capital letter.

Proofread the paragraph below. Then rewrite the paragraph on the lines provided.

    Some of the clearer water in the world is around the cayman islands. The water in the cayman area is blueer than the water in the gulf of mexico. These islands in the caribbean sea were settled by british people. Divers see some of the ocean's prettyest fish in the caribbean region.

_____

_____

_____

_____

_____

Comparing with More and Most

> • For long adjectives, use *more* and *most* to compare people, places, or things.
>
> • Use *more* to compare two people, places, or things.
>
> • Use *most* to compare more than two.

Write *more* or *most* to complete each sentence correctly.

1. To Joanna Cole, science is the ————— interesting of all subjects.

2. Joanna does the ————— careful research that she can do.

3. Her dummy is ————— organized at the beginning than at the end of her research.

4. The scientist was ————— experienced with snakes than Joanna.

5. A snakeskin is one of the ————— transparent of all animal skins.

6. Joanna's cat thought a snakeskin was ————— exciting than a nap.

7. The snakeskin was probably the ————— fascinating thing Taffy had ever seen.

8. Joanna was ————— worried than the scientist about the snakeskin.

9. Joanna learned that the workers are the ————— hard-working of all bees.

10. Joanna wondered if a tornado is ————— dangerous than a hurricane.

Extension: Ask students to write four sentences of their own, using adjectives from the above sentences. Tell students to use *more* and *most* in their sentences.

Comparing with *More* and *Most*

> • When you use *more* or *most*, do not use the ending *-er* or *-est*.

Read each sentence. Write the underlined form of each adjective correctly.

1. Sometimes for research, magazine articles are <u>more usefuler</u>

   _____ than science books.

2. Often experts are the <u>most helpfulest</u> _____ people when

   Joanna has questions.

3. She may find <u>more recenter</u> _____ information in a computer

   than in an encyclopedia.

4. Maybe a video will give the <u>most currentest</u> _____ news about a

   science topic.

5. Joanna may find <u>more scientificer</u> _____ books in a library than

   in a bookstore.

6. The <u>most importantest</u> _____ thing Joanna does before writing

   is read.

Extension: Have students make up oral sentences,
using *more* and *most* with the following adjectives:
helpful, recent, important, valuable.

Grade 4/Unit 4
On the Bus with Joanna Cole
6

Comparing with *More* and *Most*

> - For long adjectives, use *more* and *most* to compare people, places, or things.
> - Use *more* to compare two people, places, or things.
> - Use *most* to compare more than two.
> - When you use *more* or *most*, do not use the ending *-er* or *-est*.

Rewrite each sentence. Use the correct form for the adjective.

1. Hoy thinks bees would be a most difficult subject to study than snakes.

   _____

2. Elena thinks a snakebite would be dangerouser than a bee sting.

   _____

3. Lita feels that tornadoes are more harmfuler to people than snakes.

   _____

4. Kara believes that a storm would be the most challengingest topic of all.

   _____

5. Of the three subjects, David feels bees would be the more interesting.

   _____

6. Last year, the science fair was the popularest event at school.

   _____

6 | Grade 4/Unit 4
On the Bus with Joanna Cole

Extension: Encourage students to recall times when the weather was especially extreme. Invite students to describe the conditions in oral sentences, using -er, -est, more, and most.

117

Using *More* and *Most*

> • Never add *-er* and *more* to the same adjective.
>
> • Never add *-est* and *most* to the same adjective.

Read each sentence. Write the correct form of the adjective in parentheses.

1. Maple leaves are (flat) _____ than pine needles.

2. I think maple leaves are the (beautiful) _____ of all tree leaves.

3. In the wintertime, maple trees are (bare) _____ than evergreens.

4. Most encyclopedia articles are (serious) _____ than magazine articles.

5. Joanna's books are the (entertaining) _____ science books I have ever read.

6. My first science report was (boring) _____ than my latest report.

Extension: Have students make a chart, listing the six adjectives from the above sentences, then writing their comparative and superlative forms.

Grade 4/Unit 4
On the Bus with Joanna Cole

6

McGraw-Hill School Division

Comparing with *More* and *Most*

A. In each sentence, find the adjective that compares. Circle your answer.

1. Snakes are more common in the warmer parts of the world than in the colder parts.

  a snakes

  b more common

  c warmer parts

  d colder parts

2. The most likely place to find a diamondback rattlesnake in the United States is in the southeastern states.

  a most likely

  b place

  c rattlesnake

  d southeastern states

3. The black Indian cobra is one of the most poisonous of all snakes.

  a black

  b cobra

  c most poisonous

  d all snakes

B. Choose the correct adjective to complete each sentence. Circle your answer.

4. The ribbon snake is a ___ snake than the common garter snake.

  a colorfuler

  b colorfulest

  c more colorful

  d most colorful

5. Of the many reptiles, the snake has the ___ way of moving.

  a unusual

  b unusualer

  c more unusual

  d most unusual

6. One of the ___ things a snake does is shed its skin.

  a amazingest

  b amazingiest

  c more amazing

  d most amazing

Comparing with *More* and *Most*

- For long adjectives, use *more* and *most* to compare people, places, or things.
- Use *more* to compare two people, places, or things.
- Use *most* to compare more than two.

Mechanics

- Never add *-er* and *more* to the same adjective.
- Never add -est and *most* to the same adjective.

Work with a partner. Listen as your partner reads the sentences aloud.
Look for mistakes in adjectives that compare. Write the sentences
correctly. Then read them aloud.

1. Studying in bed is more unusualer than working at a desk.

   _____

2. A big dog would cause most crumpled papers than a little dog.

   _____

3. After reading several things, Joanna chooses the more interesting facts.

   _____

4. I think the most amusingest part of Joanna's story is what her cat did.

   _____

Comparing with *Good*

> - Use *better* to compare two people, places, or things.
> - Use *best* to compare more than two.

Write *better* or *best* to complete each sentence correctly.

1. Tom says "The Earliest Animals" is the ——————— article he has ever read.

2. Rosa thinks "Troubled Tongues" is a ——————— story than "The Earliest Animals."

3. To Kim, the article about mazes is the ——————— article of the three.

4. Tom thinks *Wiwaxia* is the ——————— creature of all the Cambrian animals.

5. Rosa says that *Ottoia* is a ——————— animal than *Wiwaxia*.

6. Kim believes the five-eyed creature is a ——————— creature than *Wiwaxia*.

7. Tom thinks sharp spines give ——————— protection than five eyes.

8. Rosa says that a snout is ——————— than a nose like a hose.

8 Grade 4/Unit 4
Earth's First Creatures

Extension: Have students read an article in a newspaper or magazine and circle each use of *better* or *best*.

121

Comparing with *Bad*

> - Use *worse* to compare two people, places, or things.
> - Use *worst* to compare more than two.

Write *worse* or *worst* to complete each sentence correctly.

1. Kim thinks a meteor is a ——————— disaster than an earthquake.

2. Rosa thinks an ice age would have caused ——————— changes than an earthquake.

3. What is the ——————— thing that happens during an earthquake?

4. Would a change in Earth's atmosphere be ——————— than an earthquake?

5. Tom thinks a meteor crash would have been ——————— than cold weather.

6. Which of the three events do you think would have been the ——————— one?

7. The time before the Cambrian Period was a ——————— time for animals to develop than the Cambrian Period.

8. Crushing food is not a ——————— way of eating than sucking food.

Extension: Arrange students in pairs. Ask each student to write two sentences, one with *worse* and one with *worst*. Then have students read the sentences to their partner, saying "blank" in place of *worse* and *worst*. Partners fill in the blanks.

Comparing with *Good* and *Bad*

> - Use *better* to compare two people, places, or things.
> - Use *best* to compare more than two.
> - Use *worse* to compare two people, places, or things.
> - Use *worst* to compare more than two.

Rewrite each sentence with the correct adjective from the parentheses.

1. Fossils are one of the (best, goodest) ways to learn about early animals.

_____

2. The earlier animals had (worse, worser) body systems than the Cambrian animals.

_____

3. Changes in atmosphere might have been a (worse, worst) event than weather changes.

_____

4. The (best, better) result of all the changes in environment was the "Cambrian explosion."

_____

5. One of the (worst, worsest) problems in studying early animals is their microscopic size.

_____

6. Which do you think is a (gooder, better) way of moving, floating or crawling?

_____

Extension: Arrange students in small groups. Have each group write *better, best, worse, worst* on cards and turn the cards facedown. Ask students to take turns drawing a card and using the adjective on the card in an oral sentence.

Using Commas

> - Use a comma to set off a person's name when the person is spoken to directly.
> - Use a comma after introductory words such as *yes, no,* and *well.*

Insert commas where they belong in each sentence.

1. Akiko do you know what *Wiwaxia* used to defend itself?

2. Yes it used the sharp spines that covered its body.

3. Was *Wiwaxia* the creature Jeff that hid at the bottom of the sea?

4. No the animal that hid was *Ottoia*.

5. Were the earliest animals visible Derrick?

6. Well they were not visible without a microscope.

7. Do you think Olga a period of 5 million to 10 million years is a long time?

8. Well it's not long if you're talking about the history of Earth.

124

Extension: Ask partners to work together to write questions and answers about the earliest creatures. Tell students to use their partner's name in their questions and *yes, no,* and *well* in their answers.

Grade 4/Unit 4
Earth's First Creatures
8

Comparing with *Good* and *Bad*

A. Read each sentence. Write *yes* if the underlined adjective is the correct form of *good*. Write *no* if it is not correct.

1. I think a scientist is the <u>better</u> job a person could have. _____

2. Which of the two drawings of creatures is the <u>best</u> one? _____

3. Legs are <u>better</u> body parts to walk on than spikes. _____

4. Of all the explanations for the Cambrian Period, which is the <u>best</u> one?

   _____

B. Read each sentence. Decide if the missing adjective is *worse* or *worst*. Write it on the line.

5. My drawing of *Anomalocaris* was the _____ picture I ever drew.

6. I had a _____ time drawing *Hallucigenia* than *Ottoia*.

7. I thought my drawings of Cambrian animals were the _____ ones in the

   class.

8. Then my teacher said that his drawings were _____ than mine.

Comparing with *Good* and *Bad*

> • Use *better* to compare two people, places, or things.
>
> • Use *best* to compare more than two.
>
> • Use *worse* to compare two people, places, or things.
>
> • Use *worst* to compare more than two.

Mechanics:

> • Use a comma to set off a person's name when the person is spoken to directly.
>
> • Use a comma after introductory words such as *yes, no,* and *well.*

Read the sentences about the picture. Correct the adjectives that are not written correctly. Insert commas where they belong.

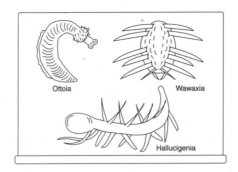

1. Jen did *Hallucigenia* or *Ottoia* have the best jaw?

_____

2. Len which of the early animals had the better legs?

_____

3. Which of the animals Harry do you think had the worse spines?

_____

4. Mary is hot weather worst than cold weather for animals?

_____

Adjectives

Read each passage and look at the underlined sentences. Is there a mistake? If there is, how do you correct it? Circle your answer.

> The photographer Jim Brandenburg thinks arctic animals are magnificent. On one of his trips, he met Scruffy. Scruffy was a wolf that took charge of[1] several playful pups. The pups thought Scruffy was nice. They made Scruffy feel important.[2]

1. **A** Add capitalization.
   B Add punctuation.
   C Use a better adjective.
   D No mistake.

2. **F** Add capitalization.
   G Add punctuation.
   H Use a better adjective.
   J No mistake.

> My teacher asked, "why did gluskabe go to see the Snow Bird?"[3] I said that he went to see him because he made snow. Gluskabe wanted the Snow Bird to sometimes make the snow light. Skunk thought the Snow Bird was an beautiful bird.[4]

3. **A** Add capitalization.
   B Add punctuation.
   C Change the article.
   D No mistake.

4. **F** Add capitalization.
   G Add punctuation.
   H Change the article.
   J No mistake.

> Sylvia Earle has dived in a Jim Suit and in a small sub. Her dive in the Jim Suit was the deepest dive ever done when not connected to a boat.[5] The suit, invented by a british diver, provided another way to explore the sea.[6]

5. **A** Add capitalization.
   B Add punctuation.
   C Use correct form of adjective.
   D No mistake.

6. **F** Add capitalization.
   G Add punctuation.
   H Use correct form of adjective.
   J No mistake.

Adjectives

Joanna Cole writes science books. <u>When she does research, she finds that a dummy is useful than index cards.</u> (7) I read her book about snakes. <u>I think it is the interesting book I've ever read.</u> (8)

---

7. **A** Adjective needs an ending.

   B Adjective needs *more*.

   C Adjective needs *most*.

   D No mistake.

8. **F** Adjective needs an ending.

   G Adjective needs *more*.

   H Adjective needs *most*.

   J No mistake.

There are several reasons why Cambrian creatures may have developed. <u>My friend asked, "Is hot weather the better explanation?"</u> (9) I answered, "No hot <u>weather would cause worse conditions than cold weather.</u> (10) Cold weather, however, might have made it happen."

---

9. **A** Punctuation

   B Incorrect use of *better* or *best*

   C Incorrect use of *worse* or *worst*

   D No mistake

10. **F** Punctuation

   G Incorrect use of *better* or *best*

   H Incorrect use of *worse* or *worst*

   J No mistake

Pronouns

> - A **pronoun** is a word that takes the place of one or more nouns.
> - A pronoun must match the noun it refers to.
> - Singular pronouns are *I, you, he, she, it, me, him, her.*
> - Plural pronouns are *we, you, they, us, them.*

Underline the incorrect pronoun in each sentence. Then write the correct pronoun on the line provided.

1. The plants were dug up, and something had nibbled it. ————

2. Don Emicho built a trap, and then it went to bed. ————

3. Don Emicho was asleep, but screeching woke them up. ————

4. When he went to the trap, they found a guinea pig. ————

5. The fox asked guinea pig why she was tied up. ————

6. The guinea pig tied up the fox as tightly as I could. ————

7. The fox told the story the guinea pig told you. ————

8. The fox knew the guinea pig had tricked us. ————

9. The fox caught the guinea pig while she was resting. ————

10. The fox was so frightened that they jumped in the hole. ————

Extension: Have students find three sentences from the story that use pronouns. Have them write the sentences down and then circle the pronoun and its referent.

Pronouns

> - A **pronoun** is a word that takes the place of one or more nouns.
>
> - A pronoun must match the noun it refers to.
>
> - Singular pronouns are *I, you, he, she, it, me, him, her.*
>
> - Plural pronouns are *we, you, they, us, them.*

Write the pronoun that correctly replaces the underlined noun in each sentence.

1. Don Emicho built a trap and put <u>the trap</u> in the field. ————

2. A beast dug up the plants and nibbled <u>the plants</u>. ————

3. Don Emicho got up when <u>Don Emicho</u> heard screeching. ————

4. The trap worked! <u>The trap</u> caught the guinea pig. ————

5. The fox asked the guinea pig how <u>the guinea pig</u> got caught. ————

6. Don Emicho was mad when <u>Don Emicho</u> found the fox. ————

7. The fox told the story the guinea pig had told <u>the fox</u>. ————

8. The fox looked for the guinea pig and found <u>the guinea pig</u> asleep. ————

9. The fox realized how the guinea pig had tricked <u>the fox</u>. ————

10. The fox was so easy to trick, the guinea pig tricked <u>the fox</u> again. ————

Extension: Have students write their own sentences using no pronouns. Then have them exchange sentences with a partner who will rewrite the sentences, replacing some or all of the nouns with pronouns.

Grade 4/Unit 5
The Fox and the Guinea Pig (10)

Pronouns

> - A **pronoun** is a word that takes the place of one or more nouns.
> - A pronoun must match the noun it refers to.
> - Singular pronouns are *I, you, he, she, it, me, him, her*.
> - Plural pronouns are *we, you, they, us, them*.

Write the pronoun that correctly completes each sentence.

1. Don Emicho was mad when ———— found the alfalfa patch a mess.

2. ———— decided to catch the intruder who did————.

3. ———— built a big trap and put ———— in the field.

4. When the big trap didn't work, ———— built a smaller one.

5. The smaller trap worked. ———— caught a guinea pig.

6. Don Emicho grabbed the guinea pig and tied ———— to a tree.

7. The fox came along and asked the guinea pig why ———— was tied up.

8. The guinea pig was able to trick ———— because the fox loved fowl.

9. The next two times, the guinea pig tricked him because ———— was easily

   scared.

10. Foxes are considered sly and clever, but there are many folk tales in which

   ———— get tricked.

Extension: Ask students to think of another story in which a fox is tricked by its victim. Have them write a few sentences to tell about it. Then ask them to identify all the pronouns in their sentences.

Contractions

- Every sentence begins with a capital letter.

- A statement ends with a period.

- A question ends with a question mark.

	am	is	are	have	has	had	will
I	I'm			I've		I'd	I'll
he		he's			he's	he'd	he'll
she		she's			she's	she'd	she'll
it		it's			it's	it'd	it'll
we			we're	we've		we'd	we'll
you			you're	you've		you'd	you'll
they			they're	they've		they'd	they'll

Write the contraction for the underlined words in each sentence.

1. Dom Emicho was mad at the guinea pig because <u>he had</u> eaten his alfalfa.

_____

2. When Don Emicho saw the guinea pig, he thought, <u>you will</u> be sorry. _____

3. "<u>I am</u> going to make guinea pig stew with you!" _____

4. Don Emicho said, "<u>I will</u> be back," and went back to bed. _____

5. The guinea pig thought, "<u>I have</u> got to get out of here." _____

6. When the fox came by, he thought, "Maybe <u>he will</u> fall for a story." _____

7. The fox listened and then asked, "So is that why <u>you are</u> all tied up?"

_____

8. So the fox took the guinea pig's place, and now <u>he is</u> tied to the tree.

_____

Extension: Have students write three sentences about the fox in the story. Ask them to include a contraction in each sentence.

Grade 4/Unit 5
The Fox and the Guinea Pig

8

Pronouns

A. Write the pronoun that can replace the underlined word or words in each sentence.

1. The guinea pig tricked <u>the fox</u>. ———

2. <u>The guinea pig</u> told the fox about Don Emicho's daughter. ———

3. "Whoever marries <u>Don Emicho's daughter</u> will eat lots of chicken." ———

4. The fox thought that marriage would be good for <u>the fox</u>. ———

5. The fox said, "<u>The fox</u> will marry Florinda!" ———

B. Write the correct pronouns to complete these sentences.

6. The fox stood against the tree, and the guinea pig tied ——— up.

7. Don Emicho was surprised when ——— saw the fox.

8. Now ——— wouldn't be getting guinea pig stew.

9. But ——— laughed when the fox told ——— how the guinea pig had tricked ———.

10. ——— thought ——— was funny, but the fox didn't.

Pronouns and Contractions

> - A **pronoun** is a word that takes the place of one or more nouns.
>
> - A pronoun must match the noun it refers to.
>
> - Singular pronouns are *I, you, he, she, it, me, him, her.*
>
> - Plural pronouns are *we, you, they, us, them.*

Mechanics

> - A **contraction** is a shortened form of two words.
>
> - A contraction may be formed by combining a pronoun and a verb.
>
> - An apostrophe (') shows where one or more letters have been left out.

Write what you think each character is saying. Use the contraction given in your sentence.

1. GUINEA PIG: (I'm)

_____

2. FOX: (you're)

_____

3. GUINEA PIG: (it'll)

_____

4. FOX: (I'll)

_____

Subject and Object Pronouns

> • Use a **subject pronoun** as the subject of a sentence.
>
> • *I, you, he, she, it, we,* and *they* are subject pronouns.

Underline the incorrect pronouns and write the correct pronoun on the line provided.

1. The family loved Marit, and them all missed her when she died.

   _____

2. When Mom came home, her and the new dog walked every day.

   _____

3. Leslie was afraid that them wouldn't love the new dog.

   _____

4. As soon as Joel met Ursula, him and her were crazy about each other.

   _____

5. The new dog and me liked each other, too.

   _____

6. Ursula made mistakes, but Mom said them were normal.

   _____

7. Once in a while, her and the dog got lost.

   _____

8. It was weeks before Joel and me got to play with Ursula.

   _____

9. People who pet guide dogs don't realize them are working.

   _____

10. When Ursula is out of harness, it's all right if us pet her.

    _____

Extension: Have students choose three sentences from the selection that have nouns as the subjects and rewrite them, replacing the nouns with subject pronouns.

Object Pronouns

> - Use an **object pronoun** after an action verb or after a word such as *for, at, of, with,* or *to.*
>
> - *Me, you, him, her, it, us,* and *them* are object pronouns.

Underline the incorrect pronouns and write the correct pronouns on the lines provided.

1. Some blind people find a cane helps they get around alone.

   _____

2. The Seeing Eye trains dogs and then teaches people to work with it.

   _____

3. When Leslie met Ursula, she was crazy about she.

   _____

4. Ursula jumped up on he.

   _____

5. Smelly garbage cans were a problem for Mom and she.

   _____

6. When dogs pass a garbage can, they want to sniff them.

   _____

7. Guide dogs can't stop. It's important for they to stay focused.

   _____

8. Mom told my brother and I about walking on trash day.

   _____

9. Guide dogs are not pets, and strangers should not try to pet him.

   _____

10. Mom allowed we to pet Ursula only when she was out of harness.

    _____

Extension: Have students find and write five examples of sentences with object pronouns from the story *Mom's Best Friend.*

Grade 4/Unit 5
Mom's Best Friend /10

Subject and Object Pronouns

> • Use a **subject pronoun** as the subject of a sentence.
>
> • Use an **object pronoun** after an action verb or after a word such as *for, at, of, with,* or *to.*

Read the sentences below. Then write the correct pronouns in the lines provided to complete each sentence.

1. My sister and _____ met a woman on the bus.

2. _____ had a guide dog with _____.

3. My brother wanted to pet the dog, but I told _____ not to.

4. The woman heard _____ and said that _____ was right.

5. _____ said that her guide dog was doing his work.

6. If we petted the dog, _____ would have to scold _____.

7. Petting _____ could make _____ forget to do his job.

8. She and her dog trained for a month before _____ became a team.

9. Guide dogs are chosen for their jobs when _____ are puppies.

10. Their training begins when _____ are old enough to learn how to be a dependable guide.

Extension: Ask students to write three sentences about training a dog. Have them include at least one pronoun in each sentence.

Using *I* and *Me*

- Always write the pronoun *I* with a capital letter.

- Use *I* or *me* last when talking about yourself and another person.

Read each sentence below. Then rewrite the sentence on the line below using *I* and *me* properly.

1. Me and my family have a new dog.

_____

2. My mom and dad got the dog for my brother and I.

_____

3. It's up to I and my brother to take care of him.

_____

4. It's our job to train him, but Mom said her and Dad would help.

_____

5. Dad is teaching my brother and I how to housebreak the dog.

_____

6. Me and Mom will take the dog to obedience classes.

_____

7. Training a dog will be a good experience for my brother and I.

_____

8. Mom says it will teach he and I responsibility.

_____

Extension: Ask students to write three sentences telling about something they did with a sibling or a friend. Have them use the pronoun *I* or *me* in each sentence.

Grade 4/Unit 5
Mom's Best Friend
8

McGraw-Hill School Division

Subject and Object Pronouns

A. Circle the bold faced pronoun or pronouns that correctly complete the sentences.

1. My dog and **I, me** go everywhere together.

2. There is a real strong bond between **he, him** and **I, me**.

3. **He, Him** always comes when I call **he, him**.

4. After school, **he, him** is waiting by the front door for **I, me**.

5. Then **he, him** and **I, me** go for a walk.

B. Write the pronoun that completes each sentence.

6. I like it when my dog greets _____ at the door.

7. I put his leash on _____, and _____ go for a walk.

8. The walk is fun for both of _____.

9. It gives _____ the exercise _____ needs every day.

10. A dog is a big responsibility for a kid, but not too big for _____.

Subject and Object Pronouns

- Use a **subject pronoun** as the subject of a sentence.

- *I, you, he, she, it, we,* and *they* are subject pronouns.

- Use an **object pronoun** after an action verb or after a word such as *for, at, of, with,* or *to.*

- *Me, you, him, her, it, us,* and *them* are object pronouns.

Mechanics

- Always write the pronoun *I* with a capital letter.

- Use *I* or *me* last when talking about yourself and another person.

Read each of the sentences below. Then fill in the blanks with the pronouns that complete each of the sentences.

1. Bruno is a dog. _____ likes to lick _____ in the face.

2. _____ can see _____ at the window when I leave to go to school.

3. If _____ look really carefully, I can see _____ wag his tail.

4. Bruno and _____ go walking every day.

5. Aurora is a cat. _____ likes to sit with _____ on the couch.

6. Aurora is small, but _____ pushes Bruno around.

Pronoun-Verb Agreement

- A present-tense verb must agree with its subject pronoun.

- Add *-s* to most action verbs when you use the pronouns *he, she,* and *it.*

- Do not add *-s* to an action verb in the present tense when you use the pronouns *I, we, you,* and *they.*

Write the correct form of the underlined action verb to complete each sentence.

1. Chandra <u>bathe</u> ——————— the Rajah's elephants.

2. On rent collection day, the Rajah <u>take</u> ——————— rice from the people.

3. The people need more rice than he <u>leave</u> ——————— for them.

4. The next bath day, Chandra <u>walk</u> ——————— to the palace.

5. There is a guard at the gate. He <u>tell</u> ——————— her the elephants are sick.

6. Chandra <u>feel</u> ——————— sad for her beloved elephants.

7. She <u>wait</u> ——————— by the gate.

8. Doctors come to cure, but they sit and <u>feasts</u> ——————— instead.

9. Chandra <u>ask</u> ——————— the Rajah to let her see the elephants.

10. She <u>find</u> ——————— that they all have ear infections.

/10 Grade 4/Unit 5
The Rajah's Rice

Extension: Have students write three sentences to tell three ways that they use math every day.

141

Pronoun-Verb Agreement

• The verbs *have* and *be* have special forms in the present tense.

Have		**Be**	
I have	We have	I am	We are
You have	You have	You are	You are
He / She / It has	They have	He / She / It is	They are

Write the correct form of the verb underlined to complete each sentence.

1. I <u>has</u> ——————— five quarters, nine dimes, and two nickels.

2. He <u>have</u> ——————— three quarters, twelve dimes, and ten nickels.

3. Together we <u>has</u> ——————— four dollars and seventy cents.

4. You can't bathe the elephants because they <u>be</u> ——————— sick.

5. They <u>have</u> ——————— infections in their ears.

6. I <u>be</u> ——————— here to help the elephants.

7. I will clean their ears, because they <u>be</u> ——————— red and sore.

8. The Rajah's elephants are better, and he <u>be</u> ——————— happy.

9. Chandra cured them, and now she <u>be</u> ——————— a hero.

10. She <u>have</u> ——————— the chance to choose her reward.

Extension: Ask students to find three sentences with present-tense forms of *be* or *have* in the selection. Have them rewrite the sentences replacing the noun that names the subject with a pronoun.

Grade 4/Unit 5
The Rajah's Rice 10

Pronoun-Verb Agreement

- A present-tense verb must agree with its subject pronoun.

- Add -s to most action verbs when you use the pronouns *he, she,* and *it.*

- Do not add -s to an action verb in the present tense when you use the pronouns *I, we, you,* and *they.*

- The verbs *have* and *be* have special forms in the present tense.

Regular Verbs		Have		Be	
I tell	We tell	I have	We have	I am	We are
You tell	You tell	You have	You have	You are	You are
He / She / It tells	They tell	He / She / It has	They have	He / She / It is	They are

Read the sentences below. Then write the correct form of the underlined verb or verbs on the lines provided.

1. Chandra is worried about the elephants because they <u>is</u> sick. —————

2. She <u>ask</u> the Rajah if she can help them. —————

3. He <u>tell</u> her she can go ahead and try. —————

4. She <u>look</u> at the first elephant's feet, tusks, and teeth. —————

5. Then she <u>look</u> in his ear and <u>see</u> that it is infected. —————

6. She <u>bathe</u> the elephants' ears and <u>sing</u> to them. —————

7. They <u>gets</u> better and <u>greets</u> her when she comes back. —————

8. The Rajah <u>be</u> happy, and he <u>promise</u> her a reward. —————

9. She <u>are</u> clever and <u>figure</u> out a way to get all the Rajah's rice. —————

10. She <u>want</u> to give the rice back to the hungry people. —————

/10 Grade 4/Unit 5
The Rajah's Rice

Extension: Have students select a paragraph from the selection and change all of the past tense verbs to the present tense.

143

Punctuation in Dialogue

> • Use quotation marks at the beginning and end of a person's exact words.
>
> • Begin a quotation with a capital letter.
>
> • Begin a new paragraph each time a new person speaks.

Rewrite this passage correctly. Add quotation marks and capital letters where needed. Begin new paragraphs whenever necessary.

what are you doing here? the zoo keeper asked Sari. I am here because I am worried about the ducks, Sari answered. I am worried about them, too, said the zoo keeper. I need them to add beauty to my pond. please let me see them. maybe I can help, said Sari. Go ahead, said the zoo keeper. if you cure them, you will be a hero.

_____

_____

_____

_____

_____

_____

Extension: Ask students to work in pairs to create and write a short dialogue. Have them write the dialogue using quotation marks and proper punctuation. Have students begin a new paragraph each time the speaker changes.

Pronoun-Verb Agreement

A. Write the correct form of the underlined action verb or verbs in each sentence.

1. She <u>love</u> —————— numbers and math.

2. When she <u>climb</u> —————— stairs, she <u>count</u> —————— the steps.

3. He <u>like</u> —————— words and word games.

4. He <u>use</u> —————— ink when he <u>work</u> —————— crossword puzzles.

5. They <u>maked</u> —————— up puzzles and <u>solves</u> —————— them.

B. Write the correct form of *have* or *be* to complete each sentence.

6. I —————— a story to tell you.

7. I will tell you the story now if you —————— ready to listen.

8. It —————— about elephants long ago.

9. It happens at a time when they —————— noses instead of long trunks.

10. It tells how elephants' trunks became the way they —————— now.

Pronoun-Verb Agreement

- A present-tense verb must agree with its subject pronoun.

- Add -s to most action verbs when you use the pronouns *he, she,* and *it.*

- Do not add -s to an action verb in the present tense when you use the pronouns *I, we, you,* and *they.*

- The verbs *have* and *be* have special forms in the present tense.

Mechanics

- Use quotation marks at the beginning and end of a person's exact words.

- Begin a quotation with a capital letter.

- Begin a new paragraph each time a new person speaks.

Rewrite the following sentences in dialogue form correcting the pronoun–verb agreement and adding quotation marks where they belong.

1. I has a new pet said Jane.

_____

2. You has an elephant said Roy.

_____

3. She said she have a cute nose.

_____

4. It are not a nose. She have a trunk! he said.

_____

5. I walks her every day said Jane. She like to walk.

_____

6. What does people think when they sees her? he asked.

_____

Possessive Pronouns

- A **possessive pronoun** takes the place of a possessive noun. It shows who or what owns something.
- Some possessive pronouns are used before nouns (*my, your, his, her, its, our, your, their*).

Rewrite the underlined parts of the sentences using possessive pronouns.

1. First Yeh-Shen's mother died, and then <u>the father of Yeh-Shen</u> died also.

   _____

2. Yeh-Shen had to live with <u>Yeh-Shen's stepmother</u> and stepmother's daughter

   in <u>the home that belonged to them</u>. _____

3. The only friend Yeh-Shen had was <u>Yeh-Shen's</u> fish. _____

4. <u>Yeh-Shen's stepmother</u> found out about the fish and caught it.

   _____

5. She cooked the fish for dinner and threw <u>the fish's bones</u> on the dung heap.

   _____

6. An old man told Yeh-Shen that <u>Yeh-Shen's fish's bones</u> had power.

   _____

7. Yeh-Shen spoke to the bones of <u>the fish that had belonged to her</u>. _____

8. Yeh-Shen told the bones of <u>Yeh-Shen's desire</u> to go to the festival.

   _____

9. Soon she was dressed in an azure gown with gold slippers on <u>Yeh-Shen's</u>

   <u>feet</u>. _____

10. The spirit warned her, "Do not lose <u>the golden shoes that belong to you</u>."

    _____

/10 Grade 4/Unit 5
Yeh-Shen: A Cinderella Story
from China

Extension: Have students identify three sentences
from the story *Yeh-Shen* that contain possessive
pronouns. Have them identify the person or thing to
which the pronoun refers.

147

Possessive Pronouns

> • Some **possessive pronouns** can stand alone (*mine, yours, his, hers, its, ours, yours, theirs*).

Replace the underlined incorrect possessive pronoun in each sentence
with the correct one on the line provided.

1. Yeh-Shen had nothing that was <u>her's</u> except the fish. —————

2. When the stepmother found out, she thought, "That fish will be <u>my's</u>."

—————

3. The old man said, "The fish bones can help you. <u>Their</u> is a powerful spirit."

—————

4. "I need clothes to wear to the festival," said Yeh-Shen. "<u>My</u> will not do."

—————

5. Stepsister thought Yeh-Shen's face was familiar, but she knew the clothes

weren't <u>her</u>. —————

6. Yeh-Shen's fine clothes turned back to the rags that were <u>her's</u> before.

—————

7. A villager who found Yeh-Shen's golden shoe pretended it was <u>he's</u> and sold

it to a merchant. —————

8. The king expected the woman from the festival to come and claim it as <u>her</u>.

—————

9. Many women tried, but Yeh-Shen's feet were much smaller than <u>theres</u>.

—————

10. The king was Yeh-Shen's beloved, and she was <u>he's</u>. —————

Extension: Have students write three sentences using
the possessive pronouns: *mine, yours, ours.*

148

Grade 4/Unit 5
Yeh-Shen: A Cinderella Story
from China
10

Possessive Pronouns

> • A **possessive pronoun** takes the place of a possessive noun. It shows who or what owns something.
>
> • Some possessive pronouns are used before nouns (*my, your, his, her, its, our, your, their*).
>
> • Some possessive pronouns can stand alone (*mine, yours, his, hers, its, ours, yours, theirs*).

Read the sentences below and write the correct possessive pronoun to complete each sentence.

1. Yeh-Shen and Cinderella both had trouble with —————— stepmothers.

2. Yeh-Shen's stepmother cooked —————— fish.

3. Cinderella's stepmother made —————— do all of the chores.

4. —————— only clothes were rags.

5. Magic fish bones gave Yeh-Shen —————— beautiful clothes.

6. A fairy godmother gave Cinderella ——————.

7. Yeh-Shen and Cinderella both lost —————— slippers.

8. Yeh-Shen's King put —————— in a pavilion.

9. Cinderella's Prince tried —————— on every woman in the kingdom.

10. Which character is —————— favorite--Yeh-Shen or Cinderella?

10

Grade 4/Unit 5
Yeh-Shen: A Cinderella Story from China

Extension: Have students write two more sentences comparing Yeh-Shen and Cinderella. Make sure that they practice using pronouns to replace proper nouns.

149

Possessive Nouns and Pronouns

> - Add an apostrophe and an -s to a singular noun to make it possessive.
>
> - Add an apostrophe to make most plural nouns possessive.
>
> - Add an apostrophe and -s to form the possessive of plural nouns that do not end in -s.
>
> - Possessive pronouns do not have apostrophes.

Read the sentences below. Then replace the underlined incorrectly formed possessive nouns and pronouns with the correctly formed word on the line provided.

1. Yeh-Shens' only friend was a fish. ——————

2. Cinderellas friends were the barnyard animals. ——————

3. The powerful spirit of the fishes' bones gave Yeh-Shen her lovely gown.

   ——————

4. Yeh-Shen and Cinderella both lost their's shoes leaving the party. ——————

5. Cinderella had won the princes' heart at the ball. ——————

6. He knew the glass slipper was her's when he began his's search. ——————

7. The king had the golden slipper, but he had never seen it's owner.

   ——————

8. The tiny size and marvelous beauty sparked the kings' curiosity. ——————

9. When Yeh-Shen took her slipper, the kings men followed her home.

   ——————

10. In both stories, the main characters' fate is the same. ——————

Extension: Ask students to write about two more similarities in the story of Yeh-Shen and the story of Cinderella. Ask them to use possessive nouns and pronouns in their sentences.

Grade 4/Unit 5
Yeh-Shen: A Cinderella Story from China   10

Possessive Pronouns

Circle the letter before the possessive pronoun that correctly completes each sentence.

1. Yeh-Shen loved the fish. She shared ———— food with it every day.

  a   his

  b   our

  c   hers

  d   her

2. The stepmother ate the fish and threw ———— bones on the dung heap.

  a   their

  b   its

  c   it's

  d   your

3. An old man told Yeh-Shen about the bones and ———— magic powers.

  a   its

  b   theirs

  c   their

  d   they's

4. The stepsister asked, "Mother, doesn't she look like ———— Yeh-Shen?"

  a   hers

  b   our

  c   its

  d   her

5. The king knew that Yeh-Shen was ———— true love.

  a   his

  b   he's

  c   their

  d   your

5   Grade 4/Unit 5
Yeh-Shen: A Cinderella Story
from China   151

Possessive Pronouns

> • Some **possessive pronouns** are used before nouns (*my, your, his, her, its, our, your, their*).
>
> • Some **possessive pronouns** can stand alone (*mine, yours, his, hers, its, ours, yours, theirs*).

Mechanics

> • Add an apostrophe and an *-s* to a singular noun to make it possessive.
>
> • Add an apostrophe to make most plural nouns possessive.
>
> • Add an apostrophe and *-s* to form the possessive of plural nouns that do not end in *-s*.
>
> • Possessive pronouns to not have apostrophes.

Read the sentences below about a fairy-tale fisherman with a magical-looking spotted fish in his fishing net. Then rewrite each sentence replacing the underlined possessive pronouns with possessive nouns.

1. His eyes opened wide with surprise.

   _____

2. Its tremendous size made it almost too big for the net.

   _____

3. Its mouth opened, and the sound that came out was music to his ears.

   _____

   _____

Read the sentences below about a fairy godmother waving her wand over an old female dog in Cinderella's back yard. Then rewrite each sentence replacing the underlined possessive pronouns with possessive nouns.

4. After one wave of her wand, her eyes started to sparkle.

   _____

   _____

5. Then a sprinkle of her magic dust made her coat lustrous and silky.

   _____

   _____

Pronouns and Homophones

- *Its, their,* and *your* are possessive pronouns.

- *It's, they're,* and *you're* are contractions meaning *it is, they are,* and *you are.*

- Do not confuse possessive pronouns with contractions that sound the same.

Read each sentence below. Then choose and circle the correct bold faced word to complete each sentence.

1. People should know how **their they're** activities affect coral reefs.

2. If you live near a coral reef, **your you're** actions could damage the reef.

3. If **your you're** aware of how delicate a reef is, you can help save them.

4. Too much fishing around a reef can affect **its it's** condition.

5. Reefs have a function; **their they're** not just beautiful.

6. A reef is safety. **Its It's** a place for small fish to hide.

7. **Its It's** also a barrier that protects the shoreline from storms.

8. **Your You're** familiar with the famous reef in Australia.

9. **Its It's** name is Great Barrier.

10. Coral reefs need plants. Plants are **their they're** food supply.

11. When reefs get outgrown with plants, **their they're** smothered.

12. Did this article add to **your you're** knowledge of coral reefs?

12 | Grade 4/Unit 5
Can We Rescue the Reefs?

Extension: Ask students to write three sentences using a homophone in each one--for example, *They're their own worst critics.*

153

Homophones

> - The word *there* means "in that place."
> - It is easy to confuse the words *there, their,* and *they're* because they sound alike.

Read each sentence below. Then replace the incorrect underlined homophones in the sentences and write the correct ones on the lines provided.

1. I have never been to Australia, but I would love to go <u>they're</u>. ————

2. The Great Barrier Reef is located <u>their</u>. ————

3. Koala bears live there, too, and <u>their</u> my favorite animal. ————

4. I love <u>they're</u> furry ears and <u>there</u> shiny black noses. ————

5. <u>They're</u> are kangaroos in Australia, too. ————

6. <u>There</u> animals I like a lot, too. ————

7. <u>Their</u> are kangaroos all over Australia. ————

8. <u>There</u> as prevalent <u>their</u> as deer are in some parts of the U.S. ————

9. Some people think <u>their</u> a real nuisance. ————

10. Suppose you're looking in your backyard and you see a kangaroo <u>they're</u>.

————

Extension: Challenge students to write a sentence that includes the three homophones *there, their,* and *they're.*

Grade 4/Unit 5
Can We Rescue the Reefs?

10

Pronoun and Contraction Homophones

- *Its, their,* and *your* are possessive pronouns.

- *It's, they're,* and *you're* are contractions meaning *it is, they are,* and *you are*.

- The word *there* means "in that place." It sounds just like *their* and *they're*.

Write the homophone that correctly completes each sentence.

1. their   they're   there

Coral reefs are smothered if ————— covered by seaweed.

2. Its   It's

————— hard to imagine that chopping down a tree can harm a reef.

3. its   it's

When a tree is cut, the soil around ————— roots is loosened.

4. Its   It's

————— washed into rivers and ends up in the sea.

5. their   they're   there

The soil in the sea harms corals by blocking ————— sunlight.

6. your   you're

Do you think about how————— actions affect the environment?

7. your   you're

When ————— running down a sand dune, what are you harming?

8. its   it's

If you take a wildflower from ————— natural spot, what could happen?

9. their   they're   there

If you take over ————— habitat, what will happen to wild animals?

10. their   they're   there

People must think about the consequences of what ————— doing.

10

Grade 4/Unit 5
Can We Rescue the Reefs?

Extension: Have students work with partners and take turns dictating and writing sentences that include the homophones *its, it's, your, you're, their, they're, there*.

155

Contractions and Possessives

> - An apostrophe takes the place of letters left out of a contraction.
> - Possessive pronouns do not have apostrophes.
> - Do not confuse possessive nouns with contractions.

A. Read the sentences below. Then replace the underlined incorrect contraction or possessive pronouns and write them correctly on the line provided.

1. People should share the world with animals because <u>its there's</u>, too.

   _____

2. <u>Their</u> all around, and you can observe them if <u>your</u> interested.

   _____

3. Next time <u>your</u> in a park or the woods, look for <u>they're</u> signs.

   _____

4. If <u>your</u> very still, <u>its</u> easy to keep an animal from noticing you.

   _____

5. But stay downwind, or <u>it's</u> keen sense of smell will catch <u>you're</u> scent.

   _____

B. Read each sentence below. Then decide if the underlined word in each sentence is a possessive noun or a contraction. Write your answer on the line provided.

6. The <u>world's</u> coral reefs are in danger of dying. _____

7. The <u>world's</u> more interesting because of coral reefs. _____

8. <u>Coral's</u> an amazing creature. _____

9. The jellyfish is the <u>coral's</u> cousin. _____

10. A coral <u>reef's</u> made up of colonies of these creatures. _____

Extension: Have students choose a singular noun and use it as both a possessive and as part of a contraction.

Grade 4/Unit 5
Can We Rescue the Reefs?

10

Possessive Pronouns and Contractions

A. Read the sentences below. Then write either the bold faced possessive pronoun or contraction above the paragraph that correctly completes the sentences on the line provided.

its   it's

    This coral is interesting. The most interesting thing about it is ————— shape. There's a coral that looks like a whip. ————— called *whip coral*. How do you think it got ————— name?

your you're

    Pretend that ————— diving on a coral reef. ————— amazed by all the fish you see. Fish of every color and shape are right before ————— eyes.

their they're   there

    ————— are about 2,500 different kinds of coral. ————— all different shapes, and ————— names sometimes come from ————— shapes. ————— is brain coral and whip coral. ————— is also sea pansy, sea pen, and organpipe coral.

Possessives and Contractions

- *Its, their,* and *your* are possessive pronouns.
- *It's, they're,* and *you're* are contractions meaning *it is, they are,* and *you are.*
- The word *there* means "in that place." It sounds just like *their* and *they're.*

Mechanics

- An apostrophe takes the place of letters left out of a contraction.
- Possessive pronouns do not have apostrophes.

Use the bold faced words above each paragraph to complete the sentences.

its it's

I like angelfish. _____ a fish that might live in a coral reef. _____

body is flat, and _____ almost round. It has an eye on each side of

_____ head.

their they're   there

_____ are lots of fish that live in coral reefs. Sometimes _____

enemies. Little fish hide from _____ enemies in the coral. _____ are

lots of hiding places in a coral reef.

your you're

Pretend _____ exploring a coral reef. Draw a picture to show what you

might see on _____ dive.

McGraw-Hill School Division

Pronouns

Read each passage. Then choose the pronoun or pronouns that belong in each space. Circle your answer.

The fox has a reputation for being sly and clever, but __(1)__ is not clever in this story. The guinea pig tricks __(2)__ several times. This story is part of a tradition of stories in which the animal that is often the victim becomes a trickster.

---

1. **A** he

    B they

    C you

    D I

2. **F** me

    G you

    H him

    J them

The Rajah has more rice than he needs. __(3)__ takes rice from the people and leaves them with too little. __(4)__ don't have enough to feed themselves. When Chandra has the chance, she chooses a reward that will solve this problem.

---

3. **A** He

    B She

    C They

    D We

4. **F** He

    G She

    H They

    J We

Pronouns

> A fairy godmother grants Cinderella's wish, but Yeh-Shen's is granted by the bones of __(5)__ fish. The old man who tells Yeh-Shen what happened to her fish also tells her about its bones and __(6)__ wish-granting powers.

5. **A** her

   B hers

   C theirs

   D they're

6. **F** her

   G hers

   H theirs

   J their

> __(7)__ clear that some human activity can have a harmful effect on nature. It is important to think about the impact __(8)__ own actions will have on the world around you.

7. **A** Its

   B It's

   C They're

   D Their

8. **F** you're

   G their

   H they're

   J your

> Rivers, streams, sand dunes, and coral reefs are all delicate in __(9)__ own way. We must all care about the future of these natural places if __(10)__ going to survive.

9. **A** they're

   B their

   C there

   D theirs

10. **F** they're

    G their

    H there

    J theirs

Grade 4/Unit 5
Make a Plan 10

Adverbs That Tell How

- An **adverb** is a word that tells more about a verb.

- Some adverbs tell how an action takes place.

- Most adverbs that tell how end in *-ly*. They are formed by adding *-ly* to an adjective.

A. Underline the adverb in each sentence.

1. In the 1940s, few Americans openly opposed racial segregation.

2. People were generally willing to let things stay as they were.

3. Many people believed that everyone should be treated equally.

4. They might have acted on their belief without stating it publicly.

5. There were groups that reacted violently to the idea of equality.

B. Add *-ly* to the bold faced word before each sentence to form an adverb that completes the sentence.

6. **significant**   Branch Rickey changed baseball —————.

7. **strong**   He felt ————— that his team should have the best players, regardless of color.

8. **careful**   He looked ————— for just the right player.

9. **exact**   He found ————— the man he was looking for in Jackie Robinson.

10. **successful**   He believed Jackie would ————— break the color barrier.

10   Grade 4/Unit 6
Teammates

EXTENSION: Ask students to write three sentences that include -ly adverbs.

161

Adverbs That Tell When or Where

- Some **adverbs** tell *when* or *where* an action takes place.
- Adverbs that tell *when* include *first, always, next, after, tomorrow, soon, early, today, then, yesterday*.
- Adverbs that tell *where* include *there, outside, up, here, nearby, ahead, around, far, away, everywhere*.

A. Rewrite each sentence by adding an adverb that tells *when*, and then underline the adverb you include.

1. Jackie Robinson played with the Dodgers' farm team, the Montreal Royals.

_____

2. He was moved up to play with the Brooklyn Dodgers.

_____

3. No matter what happened, Jackie Robinson remained calm.

_____

4. He earned the respect of his fellow players.

_____

B. Rewrite each sentence by adding an adverb that tells *where*, and then underline the adverb you include.

5. Negro League teams traveled in their own cars and buses.

_____

6. Their fans were loyal and would travel to see a game.

_____

7. Hotels would tell them they couldn't stay.

_____

8. At restaurants they would hear, "You can't eat."

_____

Extension: Ask students to identify and write three sentences from the selection that include adverbs. Have them decide if each adverb tells *how, when,* or *where*.

Grade 4/Unit 6
Teammates /8

McGraw-Hill School Division

Adverbs

- An **adverb** is a word that tells more about a verb
- Some adverbs tell *how* an action takes place.
- Some adverbs tell *when* an action takes place.
- Some adverbs tell *where* an action takes place.

Underline the adverb in each sentence. Then tell if the adverb tells *how, when,* or *where* the action takes place.

1. Jackie Robinson ran out onto the field. —————

2. What happened next hurt him deeply. —————

3. Some fans were enthusiastically cheering for him. —————

4. Some fans were booing at him loudly. —————

5. Soon the players on the other team started calling him names. —————

6. His teammates stood by and said nothing in his defense. —————

7. Jackie Robinson calmly took it all without getting angry. —————

8. His dignity quickly earned him his teammates' respect. —————

9. Pee Wee Reese bravely set the example. —————

10. He walked over and put his arm around Jackie's shoulders. —————

11. Then the jeering crowd was silent. —————

12. Afterward the Dodgers became a team in the true sense. —————

Extension: Have students write three sentences: one with an adverb that tells how, one with an adverb that tells when, and another with an adverb that tells where.

Using *Good* and *Well*

- *Good* is an adjective and is used to describe nouns.

- *Well* is an adverb that tells *how* about a verb.

- Do not confuse the adjective *good* with the adverb *well*.

A. Read each sentence below and find the word *good* or *well* used incorrectly. Then write what the correct word is on the line provided.

1. Pee Wee Reese proved himself a courageous man and a well friend.

_____

2. Jackie Robinson played good in spite of the abuses he suffered. _____

3. Pee Wee Reese was a well man who believed in doing the right thing.

_____

4. Reese's action is a well example of fairness and sportsmanship. _____

5. He said if Jackie played good enough to take his job, he deserved it.

_____

B. Complete each sentence by writing the word *good* or *well* on the line provided.

6. Branch Rickey wanted _____ players on the Dodgers.

7. If a man played _____, the color of his skin didn't matter.

8. He thought Jackie Robinson would handle himself _____ on the field.

9. Reacting to the insults or fighting back would not be a _____ thing.

10. For Jackie, behaving _____ was the best revenge.

Extension: Have students write two sentences using the adjective *good* and two sentences using the adverb *well*.

Grade 4/Unit 6
Teammates 10

Adverbs

Read each sentence. Then using the clue in the parentheses, circle the letter before the adverb that completes each sentence.

1. The Dodgers played ___ . (when?)
   a. here
   b. yesterday
   c. enthusiastically
   d. the Reds

2. Jackie Robinson changed the game of baseball ___. (how?)
   a. then
   b. there
   c. permanently
   d. everywhere

3. His success was a victory for black athletes ___. (where?)
   a. today
   b. forever
   c. then
   d. everywhere

4. He gave black athletes the opportunity to compete ___. (how?)
   a. equally
   b. today
   c. anywhere
   d. nearby

5. There are African American heroes in all sports ___. (when?)
   a. today
   b. everywhere
   c. internationally
   d. successfully

6. Some of the fans treated Jackie Robinson ___. (how?)
   a. next
   b. later
   c. cruelly
   d. before

Adverbs

- An **adverb** is a word that tells more about a verb.

- Some adverbs tell *how* an action takes place.

- Most adverbs that tell *how* end in *-ly*. They are formed by adding *-ly* to an adjective.

Mechanics

- *Good* is an adjective and is used to describe nouns.

- *Well* is an adverb that tells how about a verb.

- Do not confuse the adjective *good* with the adverb *well*.

Read each sentence below. Then write the correct form of the underlined word on the line provided.

1. The pitcher wound up and threw the ball <u>powerful</u>. _____

2. The ball went flying <u>swift</u> toward the batter. _____

3. The batter <u>brief</u> felt a moment of panic. _____

4. Then he held the bat <u>tight</u> and swung as hard as he could. _____

5. The ball rose high into the air and arched <u>graceful</u> over the left field wall.

_____

Adverbs That Compare

- An **adverb** can compare two or more actions.

- Add -er to short adverbs to compare two actions.

- Add -est to short adverbs to compare more than two actions.

Add -er or -est to each boldfaced adverb to complete the sentences below. Remember to drop the final e or change y to i when necessary before adding -er and -est.

1. near She walked ——————— to look into the silver cage.

2. close The ——————— she came, the sadder the yellow bird appeared to be.

3. early The princess rose ——————— than the rest of the household.

4. low The lady-in-waiting bowed low, but the governess bowed ———————.

5. high Of all the birds in flight, the little yellow one flew ———————.

6. loud When it sang, it sang ——————— and best.

7. straight The princess stood ——————— after she defied the queen.

8. deep She breathed ——————— and laughed more.

9. fast Sliding over the snow, the princess went ——————— and farthest.

10. soon The ——————— people learn to enjoy simple things, the better they will be.

Extension: Have students work with a partner to find examples of adverbs with -er or -est in this selection and others.

Adverbs That Compare

> - Use *more or most* to form comparisons with adverbs that end in *–ly* or with longer adverbs.
>
> - Use *more* to compare two actions.
>
> - Use *most* to compare more than two actions.
>
> - When you use *more* or *most*, do not use the ending *-er* or *-est*.

Use *more* or *most* with the underlined adverb in each first sentence, to complete the two sentences that follow.

1. A lark sings <u>sweetly</u> in the morning.

   Some think a nightingale sings _____ in the evening.

   But the princess's little yellow bird sang _____.

2. The children laughed <u>joyfully</u> as they played in the snow.

   They laughed _____ when they saw the yellow bird.

   However, they cheered and laughed _____ when the princess

   came out to play with them.

3. The lady-in-waiting spoke <u>harshly</u> about the other children.

   The governess spoke _____ about them.

   The queen spoke of them _____ of all.

4. The princess told the lady-in-waiting <u>firmly</u>, "That's not true."

   She told the governess _____, "That's not true."

   She told the queen _____, "That's not true."

5. The iron fence <u>effectively</u> separated the princess from other children.

   Vines _____ shut her off from the children.

   They isolated her _____ after they had grown tall and thick.

Extension: Have students look in stories and magazine articles to find examples of comparative adverbs formed with *more* or *most*.

Grade 4/Unit 6
The Malachite Palace / 5

Adverbs That Compare

- An **adverb** can compare two or more actions.
- Add *-er* to short adverbs to compare two actions.
- Add *-est* to short adverbs to compare more than two actions.
- Use *more* or *most* to form comparisons with adverbs that end in *–ly* or with longer adverbs.
- Use *more* to compare two actions.
- Use *most* to compare more than two actions
- When you use *more* or *most*, do not use the ending *-er* or *-est*.

Write the comparative form of the adjective given to complete each sentence.

1. sadly

On the balcony the bird sang again, but ——————— than it had before.

2. brightly

Whenever the children laughed, the bird would sing ——————— than before.

3. beautifully

The bird sang ——————— than other birds.

4. thickly

When summer came, the vines covered the iron fence ——————— than in the winter.

5. loud

The more the children laughed, the ——————— the yellow bird sang.

6. loud

The bird sang ——————— when the princess laughed.

7. clumsily

At first the princess worked ——————— with the tools.

8. confidently

But after a while, she began to work ———————.

8

Grade 4/Unit 6
The Malachite Palace

Extension: Have students write three sentences that include examples of adverbs that compare.

169

Using *More* and *Most*

- Never add *-er* and *more* to the same adverb.

- Never add *-est* and *most* to the same adverb.

Write the correct adverbs on the lines provided.

1. Children live more happilier in the company of others. _____

2. The princess spoke most confidentliest when she said, "That's not true!"
_____

3. At the end, the yellow bird sang more louder than before. _____

4. She opened the window more wider, and the yellow bird flew in. _____

5. When the children laughed, the bird sang more brightlier. _____

6. Nobody worked with tools more clumsilier than the princess._____

7. She developed her skills more sooner than most. _____

8. She removed the door so that the bird could come and go more freelier.
_____

9. Now the cage more closelier resembled an archway. _____

10. The yellow bird returned most willingliest and brought his friends. _____

Extension: Have students write examples of comparative adverbs formed with *more* and *most* in the story *The Malachite Palace*.
170

Grade 4/Unit 6
The Malachite Palace /10

Adverbs That Compare

A. For each of the adverbs below, write the form you would use to compare two things. Then choose one of the adverbs you formed and use it in a sentence.

1. carefully —————————

2. soon —————————

3. clumsily —————————

4. patiently —————————

5. fast —————————

6. —————————————————————

B. For each of the following adverbs, write the form you would use to compare more than two things. Then choose one of the adverbs you formed and use it in a sentence.

7. loud —————————

8. actively —————————

9. soon —————————

10. early —————————

11. happily —————————

12. —————————————————————

Adverbs That Compare

- Add *-er* to short adverbs to compare two actions.

- Add *-est* to short adverbs to compare more than two actions.

- Use *more* to compare two actions.

- Use *most* to compare more than two actions.

Mechanics

- Never add *-er* and *more* to the same adverb.

- Never add *-est* and *most* to the same adverb.

Add comparative adverbs to complete the sentences below.

1. The crow sang ——————— than the songbird.

2. The songbird sang ——————— than the crow.

3. The lady-in-waiting waited ——————— than the governess.

4. The governess behaved ——————— than the lady-in-waiting.

5. The princess worked ——————— than the prince.

6. The prince worked ——————— than the princess.

Negatives

- A **negative** is a word that means "no," such as *not, never, nobody, nowhere,* and contractions with *n't.*
- Do not use two negatives in the same sentence.
- You can fix a sentence with two negatives by removing one.

Correct each sentence by removing one of the negatives. Then rewrite the sentence.

1. "I wouldn't never pay a dollar and eighty-nine cents for toothpaste."

_____

2. "Toothpaste isn't made of no expensive ingredients."

_____

3. Rufus wasn't trying to make no money.

_____

4. He thought people shouldn't never have to pay a lot for toothpaste.

_____

5. He didn't use no secret ingredients.

_____

6. His toothpaste didn't have no special name.

_____

7. He didn't put no printing on the box.

_____

8. "I don't have no profits to pay you yet."

_____

Extension: Have students work with a partner to write and correct sentences with two negatives.

Negatives

> • You can correct a sentence with two negatives by changing one negative to a positive word.

no ——— any   nothing ——— anything   no one ——— anyone

never ——— ever   nobody ——— anybody   nowhere ——— anywhere

Correct these sentences by changing one negative word to a positive word.

1. "I don't think nobody should pay a lot for toothpaste."

   _____

2. The main ingredient isn't nothing but baking soda.

   _____

3. No one would never think three cents was too much for toothpaste.

   _____

4. You can't find cheaper toothpaste nowhere.

   _____

5. No one never turned down a chance to be a stockholder.

   _____

6. Kate had never seen nothing more beautiful than that machine.

   _____

7. "We don't exactly lend money to just nobody," said Mr. Perkell.

   _____

8. Our toothpaste doesn't have nothing like a fancy name or a fancy box.

   _____

Extension: Ask students to work with partners to write sentences including the negatives *no, never, nothing, nobody, no one,* and *nowhere.* Have them exchange their sentences with a partner, who will correct the sentence by changing the negative to a corresponding positive word: *any, ever, anything, anybody, anyone,* and *anywhere.*

Grade 4/Unit 6
The Toothpaste Millionaire

8

Negatives

- Do not use two negatives in the same sentence.
- You can fix a sentence with two negatives by removing one.
- You can correct a sentence with two negatives by changing one negative to a positive word.

Rewrite each sentence below by dropping a negative or changing one negative to a positive word.

1. There isn't no profit yet.

_____

2. *Toothpaste* doesn't make no fancy claims.

_____

3. It doesn't do nothing but clean your teeth.

_____

4. They never waste no money making it.

_____

5. Rufus doesn't have no new ideas yet.

_____

6. Rufus never had to pay his classmates nothing.

_____

7. They never worked for nothing but stock.

_____

8. There couldn't have been no better deal.

_____

Extension: Have students review the strategies they used to correct the sentences on this page. Then have students try to correct each sentence by using the other possible strategy.

Contractions

> • A **contraction** is a shortened form of two words.
>
> • A contraction can be formed by combining a verb with the word *not*.
>
> • An apostrophe (') shows where one or more letters have been left out.

can't = cannot	*didn't = did not*	*aren't = are not*
don't = do not	*haven't = have not*	*couldn't = could not*
doesn't = does not	*wasn't = was not*	*wouldn't = would not*

Fix the following sentences with two negatives by removing the contraction of the word *not*.

1. He can't see no reason for it.

_____

2. He wouldn't never spend a lot for toothpaste.

_____

3. Doesn't he have no more good ideas?

_____

4. You aren't going nowhere.

_____

5. We couldn't do nothing to stop him.

_____

6. Compared with the usual price, three cents wasn't nothing.

_____

7. You haven't finished none of your work.

_____

8. She didn't nothing of the kind.

_____

Extension: Have students identify and list the contractions formed with *not* found in the selection, *The Toothpaste Millionaire.*

176

Grade 4/Unit 6
The Toothpaste Millionaire   8

Negatives

A. Circle the letter next to the sentence that best revises each sentence with two negatives.

1. Rufus wasn't trying to make no money.
   a   Rufus was trying to make money.
   b   Rufus wasn't trying to make money.
   c   Rufus was not trying to not make money.
   d   Rufus was trying not to make money.

2. We don't have no profits to pay anybody yet.
   a   We have profits for pay people yet.
   b   We have no profits yet to pay nobody.
   c   We don't have profits to pay nobody yet.
   d   We have no profits to pay anybody yet.

3. *Toothpaste* doesn't make no fancy claims.
   a   *Toothpaste* doesn't make any fancy claims.
   b   *Toothpaste* makes any fancy claims.
   c   *Toothpaste* never makes no fancy claims.
   d   *Toothpaste* doesn't make any claims.

4. We didn't have no other kids working with us.
   a   We didn't have any other kids working with us.
   b   We did have other kids working with us.
   c   We had other kids working with us.
   d   We never worked with other kids.

5. Isn't this not the most beautiful machine ever?
   a   Is this the most beautiful machine never?
   b   This isn't the most beautiful machine, is it?
   c   Isn't this the most beautiful machine ever?
   d   Is this a beautiful machine?

6. They don't use no expensive ingredients.
   a   They use not expensive ingredients.
   b   They use expensive ingredients.
   c   They don't use any ingredients.
   d   They don't use expensive ingredients.

Negatives

- Do not use two negatives in the same sentence.
- You can fix a sentence with two negatives by removing one.
- You can correct a sentence with two negatives by changing one negative to a positive word.

Mechanics

- A contraction is a shortened form of two words.
- A contraction can be formed by combining a verb with the word *not*.
- An apostrophe (') shows where one or more letters have been left out.

Correct the sentences, remembering the rules above, to make them describe the pictures.

1. James didn't never want to have all these peanuts.

_____

2. But he couldn't never make ten pounds of peanut butter with fewer.

_____

3. He didn't know nobody who didn't like peanut butter and jelly sandwiches.

_____

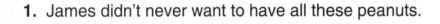

4. Kate wasn't glad when she didn't have to use baby jars anymore.

_____

5. Kate didn't think this machine could never fill toothpaste tubes.

_____

Prepositions

- A **preposition** comes before a noun or pronoun and relates that noun or pronoun to another word in a sentence.
- Common prepositions are *about, above, across, after, around, at, behind, down, for, from, in, near, of, on, over, to, under,* and *with.*

Complete each sentence by adding a preposition.

1. The selection gives information ————— whales.

2. There are many different kinds ————— whales.

3. The sperm whale can stay underwater ————— more than an hour.

4. Narwhals live ————— the Arctic.

5. Orcas are found all ————— the world.

6. Baleen plates hang ————— the whale's upper jaw.

7. Every year, gray whales migrate ————— warm Mexican waters.

8. Gray whales feed ————— the bottom of the ocean floor.

9. They fill their mouths, and then they rise ————— the surface.

10. Fin whales often work ————— partners to round up fish.

11. A humpback whale's song can be heard ————— far away.

12. When humpback whales feed, they send out clouds of bubbles ————— a

school of small fish to trap them.

Extension: Have students select a paragraph in the selection *Whales* and list the prepositions.

Prepositional Phrases

> • A **prepositional phrase** is a group of words that begins with a preposition and ends with a noun or pronoun.

Underline the prepositional phrases in the following sentences.

1. Every year, gray whales travel about ten thousand miles.

2. Blue whales strain krill through their baleen plates.

3. Toothed whales are closely related to dolphins and porpoises.

4. A narwhal has a tooth that sticks through its upper lip.

5. Orcas, or killer whales, perform in marine parks around the country.

6. Orcas eat fish and other sea mammals, but they are gentle in captivity.

7. Orcas are found in all the world's oceans.

8. Right whales used to be common in the North Atlantic Ocean.

9. In the summer, gray whales feed in cold Arctic waters.

10. In the winter, they travel ten thousand miles to warmer waters.

11. The journey of the gray whales is the longest migration of any mammal.

12. The International Whaling Commission was established in 1946.

Extension: Have students write five sentences, including at least one prepositional phrase in each sentence, about the selection *Whales*.

180

Grade 4/Unit 6
Whales

12

Prepositions and Prepositional Phrases

> • A **preposition** comes before a noun or pronoun and relates that noun or pronoun to another word in a sentence.
>
> • A **prepositional phrase** is a group of words that begins with a preposition and ends with a noun or pronoun.

Circle the preposition and then underline the prepositional phrase in each sentence.

1. There used to be many whales in the world's oceans.

2. Some whales have been hunted almost to extinction.

3. The right whale used to be common in the North Atlantic Ocean.

4. It got its name from early whalers.

5. For them, it was the "right whale" to hunt.

6. It swam slowly, and it had lots of baleen and blubber.

7. Now it is hard to find a right whale anywhere in the world.

8. A right whale has strange bumps, called callosities, on its head.

9. Each whale has its own unique pattern of bumps.

10. Scientists can identify a particular whale by its callosity pattern.

10 Grade 4/Unit 6
Whales

Extension: Ask students to write three facts about whales and have them include a prepositional phrase in each sentence.

181

Letter Punctuation

> • Begin the greeting and closing in a letter with a capital letter.
>
> • Use a comma after the greeting and the closing in a letter.
>
> • Use a comma between the names of a city and a state.
>
> • Use a comma between the day and year in a date.

Add capital letters and commas where they are needed in these letters.

12 Nightingale Lane

Portland ME 04000

August 26 2001

dear Robert

I can't wait to see you next week. I am really looking forward to our trip on the whale-watching boat. Do you really think we'll see whales?

your friend

Fred

8 Prospect Street

Portsmouth   NH 03000

September 2   2001

dear Fred

I'm looking forward to our trip, too. I hope we see some whales. There's a good chance we will. It's really exciting when it happens. See you soon.

your friend

Robert

Extension: Have students pretend that they visited a marine park and saw an orca. Have them write a short letter to a friend telling about what they saw.

Grade 4/Unit 6
Whales / 8

Prepositions and Prepositional Phrases

A. Complete each sentence below by writing the missing preposition.

1. Orcas are familiar ———— most people.

2. Many people have seen them ———— marine parks.

3. They live and perform ———— huge tanks of water.

4. They are real crowd-pleasers and are loved ———— audiences.

5. People are amazed ———— the things an orca can do.

B. Underline the prepositional phrase in each of the sentences below.

6. Baleen whales feed on small fish and krill.

7. The baleen in the whale's mouth acts like a filter.

8. Baleen whales open their mouths and skim through the water.

9. As they swim, krill is trapped by the baleen.

10. The water passes through the gaps in the baleen.

Prepositions and Prepositional Phrases

> • A **preposition** comes before a noun or pronoun and relates that noun or pronoun to another word in a sentence.
>
> • A **prepositional phrase** is a group of words that begins with a preposition and ends with a noun or pronoun.

Mechanics

> • Begin the greeting and closing in a letter with a capital letter.
>
> • Use a comma after the greeting and the closing in a letter.
>
> • Use a comma between the names of a city and a state.
>
> • Use a comma between the day and year in a date.

Add capital letters, commas, and prepositions to correct and complete this letter.

356 Lakeside Road

Orlando   Florida   32899

March 30   2001

dear Grandma

Remember the baby orca we saw when you were here last year? We went

_____ the marine park and saw it again. It performed _____ itself this time

_____ a special show. It was terrific! I wish you had been _____ us.

Love,

Andrea

Combining Sentences with Adjectives and Adverbs

> • Two sentences can be combined by adding an **adjective** or **adverb** to one sentence.

Rewrite the sentences below, using the adjective or adverb to combine them into one sentence.

1. The Everglades is in trouble. It's serious.

_____

2. Farmers use chemicals. The chemicals are dangerous.

_____

3. Everglades' animals eat plants. They are native plants.

_____

4. Some plants are invasive. They are pushing out native plants.

_____

5. The Everglades is very beautiful. It is swamplike.

_____

6. Before us is a field of tall grass. It is flat and soggy.

_____

7. An egret stands at the water's edge. It is motionless.

_____

8. Tree frogs croak. They croak noisily.

_____

9. You can tell an alligator from a crocodile. You can easily do it.

_____

10. A crocodile has a tooth that sticks out. It is long.

_____

/10 Grade 4/Unit 6
Saving the Everglades

Extension: Ask students to write two sentences and have a partner combine them into one sentence by adding an adjective or an adverb.

185

Combining Sentences with Prepositional Phrases

> • Two sentences can be combined by adding a **prepositional phrase** to one sentence.

Rewrite the sentences below, using the prepositional phrase to combine them into one sentence.

1. Large numbers of people moved. They moved to Florida.

_____

2. Engineers tried to stop flooding. They did this in the 1920s.

_____

3. Their efforts had a negative effect. The effect was on the Everglades.

_____

4. Engineers are returning the rivers. They are returning the rivers to their

original courses.

_____

5. The Everglades has been called a "river of grass." It is in Florida.

_____

6. The Everglades has been damaged. It's been damaged by people.

_____

7. People saw the Everglades just as swampland. This was true for almost a

century.

_____

8. People's thinking has changed. This has happened in recent years.

_____

Extension: Ask students to write two sentences for a
partner to combine by joining the two sentences with
a prepositional phrase.

Grade 4/Unit 6
Saving the Everglades

8

Combining Sentences

> • Two sentences can be combined by:
>   adding an **adjective** or an **adverb** to one sentence.
>   adding a **prepositional phrase** to one sentence.

Combine the pair of sentences below by adding an adjective, adverb, or prepositional phrase. Then underline what you added to join the two sentences.

1. We spent the day observing nature. We were at Everglades National Park.

_____

2. We spotted a tree frog. It was lime-green.

_____

3. The ibis glided over the water. It glided soundlessly.

_____

4. A splash attracted our attention. It happened suddenly.

_____

5. A reptile slipped into the water. It was large and greenish-brown.

_____

6. It disappeared before we could get a good look. It disappeared underwater.

_____

7. Then we noticed a tooth sticking out. It was a long tooth.

_____

8. It was a crocodile we saw. We saw it in the water.

_____

Extension: Ask students to write four more sentences telling about something they think they might see on a visit to the Everglades. Then have them combine two of them using an adjective, adverb, or prepositional phrase.

Using Punctuation Marks

- Every sentence begins with a capital letter.

- Use the correct end mark for each sentence.

- Use a comma to set off a person's name when the person is spoken to directly.

- Use a comma after introductory words such as *yes, no,* and *well.*

Make corrections to this dialogue between Max and Carrie, who are visiting Everglades National Park, by adding correct punctuation and capitalization.

Carrie: will we see wildlife if we take this trail

_____

Max: yes I think we will that's what the map shows

_____

Carrie: Max look it's a snowy egret isn't it beautiful

_____

Max: that's pretty amazing

_____

Carrie: look at all of those flamingoes have you ever seen a real one

_____

Max: no I've only seen plastic ones in people's front yards

_____

Carrie: well you're seeing the real ones now they look really different from

the plastic ones

_____

Max: yes I have to agree with you about that Carrie

_____

Extension: Have students continue writing the dialogue between the two characters visiting Everglades National Park, being sure to use the correct punctuation.

Grade 4/Unit 6
Saving the Everglades 8

McGraw-Hill School Division

Combining Sentences

Study the sentences below. Then circle the correct choice of what was added to combine the two sentences into one.

1. We stood on the boardwalk. It was wet.
   We stood on the wet boardwalk.
   - **a.** adjective
   - **b.** adverb
   - **c.** prepositional phrase

2. We stared into the water. We stared for a while.
   We stared into the water for a while.
   - **a.** adjective
   - **b.** adverb
   - **c.** prepositional phrase

3. I was certain I could see an alligator lurking. It was below the surface.
   I was certain I could see an alligator lurking below the surface.
   - **a.** adjective
   - **b.** adverb
   - **c.** prepositional phrase

4. Then we spotted another alligator. It was on the bank.
   Then we spotted another alligator on the bank.
   - **a.** adjective
   - **b.** adverb
   - **c.** prepositional phrase

5. The alligator winked an eye. It did it sleepily.
   The alligator winked an eye sleepily.
   - **a.** adjective
   - **b.** adverb
   - **c.** prepositional phrase

6. Then the alligator slithered down the bank. It moved silently.
   Then the alligator slithered silently down the bank.
   - **a.** adjective
   - **b.** adverb
   - **c.** prepositional phrase

Correcting Sentences

- Two sentences can be combined by:
    - adding an **adjective** or an **adverb** to one sentence.
    - adding a **prepositional phrase** to one sentence.

Mechanics

- Every sentence begins with a capital letter.
- Use the correct end mark for each sentence.
- Use a comma to set off a person's name when the person is spoken to directly.
- Use a comma after introductory words such as *yes, no,* and *well.*

Combine the groups of words below to form one sentence. Then add the correct sentence punctuation and capitalization.

1. do you see that crocodile   it is on the bank

   _____

2. yes I see that crocodile   it is sleepy-looking

   _____

3. the grass almost hides him   the grass is tall

   _____

4. his snout is almost in the water   it is pointy

   _____

5. do you think he sees us up here   we are on this walk

   _____

6. well my friend I don't think so   I really don't

   _____

Adverbs

Read each passage and look at the underlined sentences. Is there a better way to write or say each sentence? If there is, which is the better way? Circle your answer.

The most remarkable thing about Jackie Robinson was his ability to take insults without fighting back. <u>Crowds attacked him wordly</u>. <u>Players on the other team might try to hurt him with cleats</u>. Through it all, he never let anger get the better of him. (2)
(1)

---

1. **A** Crowds attacked him words.

   B Crowds attacked him verbally.

   C Crowds attacked him verbal.

   D No mistake.

2. **F** Players on the other team might try to hurt him physical.

   G Players on the other team might try to hurt him physically.

   H Players on the other team might try to hurt him bad.

   J No mistake.

The yellow bird sat sadly in its cage, never singing. Then one day, for no reason, the princess let it out. <u>Free again, the bird sang most sweetly than before</u>. <u>But it sang even more joyfully when the princess came out to play with the other children</u>.
(3)
(4)

---

3. **A** Free again, the bird sang most sweet.

   B Free again, the bird sang more sweeter.

   C Free again, the bird sang more sweetly than before.

   D No mistake.

4. **F** But it sang joyfully of all when the princess came out to play with the other children.

   G But it sang even more joyful when the princess came out to play with the other children.

   H But it sang even most joyfully when the princess came out to play with the other children.

   J No mistake.

Adverbs

Toothpaste <u>didn't have no fancy name</u>. Its basic ingredient was baking
soda, and it was flavored with a little peppermint oil. People loved it. <u>It didn't do</u>
<u>nothing but clean your teeth</u>.
₍₆₎

---

5. **A** Toothpaste didn't have no
kind of fancy name.

  B Toothpaste didn't have any
fancy name.

  C Toothpaste did have no
fancy name.

  D No mistake.

6. **F** It didn't do but clean your teeth.

  G It didn't do anything but clean
your teeth.

  H It did do nothing but clean your
teeth.

  J No mistake.

Orcas are also called "killer whales." <u>They can be found over most of the</u>
<u>world's oceans</u>. Many people have seen orcas, but not in the ocean. <u>They have</u>
<u>seen them around marine parks</u>.

---

7. **A** They can be found in most
of the world's oceans.

  B They can be found most of
the world's oceans.

  C They can be found over most
in the world's oceans.

  D No mistake.

8. **F** They have seen them about
marine parks.

  G They have seen them at marine
parks.

  H They have seen them from
marine parks.

  J No mistake.

We spent the day observing nature at Everglades National Park. <u>We</u>
<u>spotted a tree toad. It was lime-green.</u> We saw a white egret. <u>We saw an</u>
<u>alligator sunning itself on the bank.</u> When it heard us, it slipped into the water.

---

9. **A** We spotted a tree toad and
it was lime-green.

  B We spotted a smartly dressed
tree toad. It was lime-green.

  C We spotted a lime-green
tree toad.

  D No mistake.

10. **F** We saw an alligator sunning
itself and it was on the bank.

  G We saw an alligator lazily sunning
itself. It was at the bank.

  H We saw an alligator sunning
itself. It was on the bank.

  J No mistake.

Grade 4/Unit 6
Sorting It Out 10